to succeed...
JUST LET GO

to succeed...
JUST LET GO

WILLIE HORTON

JANUS PUBLISHING COMPANY LTD
Cambridge, England

First published in Great Britain 2006
by Janus Publishing Company Ltd
The Studio
High Green
Great Shelford
Cambridge CB22 5EG
www.januspublishing.co.uk

Reprinted 2009

Copyright © Willie Horton 2006

British Library Cataloguing-in-Publication Data
A catalogue record for this book is available from the British Library

ISBN 978-1-85756-645-1

All rights reserved. No part of this publication may be reproduced,
stored in a retrieval system or transmitted in any form or by any
means, electric, mechanical, photocopying, recording or otherwise,
without the prior permission of the publisher.

The right of Willie Horton to be identified as the author
of this work has been asserted by him in accordance with the
Copyright, Designs and Patents Act 1988.

Cover Design: Janus Publishing

Printed and bound in the UK by PublishPoint
from KnowledgePoint Limited, Reading

Contents

Introduction	vii

Part One – Understanding Yourself

You're a Robot	1
Your Reality	11
The Mechanics of Your Mind	19

Part Two – Switching Yourself On

Free Your Mind	31
Believe	45
Coming to Your Senses	57
Stop Thinking	73

Part Three – Welcome to the Real World

The Importance of Now	89
Energy and Opportunity	103
Let Go	117
Your Goals	129
Take Responsibility	147
Start Living	155

Introduction

I've been working with clients for nearly ten years, helping them awaken to the true nature of their real potential – and to achieve success that normal people would consider unbelievable. But that's, of course, why normal people are normal – most have yet to awaken to all that they can be.

My work is simple – for normal people, almost too simple. If you understand how your mind works, you can actively use it for your benefit – to get what you want out of life. By simply changing how you use your mind, you create a whole new life for yourself – one that gives you effortless success that lasts.

This book uses the same logical steps that I take with my clients. As you take each step, you are provided with simple mental exercises – again, too simple for most! But the results are more than rewarding and, even though many of my clients write glowingly of their success, the results are, in reality, beyond words.

All that is required is an open mind and a desire for a wonderful life – and, I believe, we'd all like some of that!

Willie Horton
www.XL-Yourself.org

PART ONE

Understanding Yourself

Chapter One
You're a Robot

You're Not Using the Mind God Gave You!

Right now you're using less than 2 per cent of your mind. But you can learn, with little effort, to use all of your mind. As a result, you can achieve everything your heart desires, effortlessly. And, everything you need to know is within these pages.

The standard, logical reaction to this is predictable: "If that's true, how come I don't know this already? How come everyone isn't doing it, if it's so simple?"

Only very few people know what's in this book and actually put it into practice. But, there are such people. They're a tiny minority of people – university research puts it at about 4 per cent of people. They are the spectacularly successful – life's high achievers.

Right now, if you're normal or average, you're making a living and life is "not too bad". But, you can't live your perfect day every day. Your life is broken into segments of struggle and relaxation – work and holidays – and, as far as you know, that's how it's meant to be. No-one's ever told you otherwise, have they?

In fact, you've been told the opposite. Get a good education, get a good job, get a fine house (and the mortgage that goes with it), progress in your career, work hard, play hard, retire and die. OK, that's maybe a little hard – but that's your lot, that's how it is. And when we've done, we'll tell our children pretty much the same – and so the treadmill continues.

to succeed... JUST LET GO

Right now, by virtue of your reading these words, you want something more. Some describe it as "inner peace", "happiness", "fulfilment", "peace of mind", "freedom", even "financial freedom" – but they all amount to the same thing – something more, something that raw material success or career progression does not offer.

And yet, everything you need is right before your very eyes. So, how can it be that you don't know this? How can it be that everyone doesn't know?

The fact is that, at an instinctive level, we all know – in our subconscious mind, we all know – as young children, we all knew. But the system, social convention, education, even our relationships, have pulled the wool over our eyes – and we can't see what's right before us.

The proposition in this book is beyond simplicity – simply put, by changing how you use your mind, you change your life. It takes only a tiny change in your way of thinking – yet a change that few of us have had explained to us. This tiny change in how you think is guaranteed to change your life, beyond recognition. I can confirm this from personal experience. My many clients can confirm it from their personal experience. It works. Are you interested?

The tiny change in how you think is so simple that it defies logic – so, your logical mind will say "that's too good to be true". So, in order that you understand and take on board what I am proposing, I will start by using logic!

Take a simple analogy. Picture your mind as an iceberg. Like an iceberg, part of your mind is above the water – whilst a big part floats, unseen, below the water. The part above the water is that of which we're all conscious – our conscious mind. This is the part of your mind where you do your thinking, make your decisions, learn "knowledge." – It's that part of our mind that many would believe – rightly or wrongly. would separate us from the animals .

Floating below the surface is that part of our mind of which, generally, we are not conscious – our subconscious mind that part; of our mind which has fascinated everyone from Freud on. Like the iceberg, this represents the greater part of our mind – but it is not something that has an impact on how we think or act from our conscious intelligence. Or does it?

You're a Robot

Your Operating System

You woke up this morning (or at least you got out of bed!). Put another way, you didn't die whilst you slept as a result of you not thinking about breathing whilst you were asleep. Breathing is something we do without thinking about it, isn't it. For that matter, whilst you slept last night, your heart kept beating, your food was digested and your mind (your subconscious mind) was pretty active – whilst you were dreaming. So a lot of things went on last night, whilst you were sleeping, that you didn't think about. In fact, having to think about things like that doesn't bear thinking about!!

It's as if your mind were like a computer – and just as with every computer, you were delivered with your very own "operating system", your "Windows XP", and your operating system looks after some fairly important functions, like the ones we've just mentioned, without you having to think about it.

Automatic Actions

But, again, just like that computer, you have some other "on-board functions" that are performed without the slightest conscious intervention or thought. When you got out of bed this morning, you walked – maybe to the bathroom, maybe the kitchen, maybe to the window, took one look and decided to get back into bed! – but, you went somewhere. And, did you think about the act of walking? Did you think about the complex multiple muscle movements involved in putting one foot in front of the other whilst not falling over? Of course you didn't! Yet, there was a time when you couldn't do that – you learned it (by watching people who were walking already) and you stored that program in your subconscious mind so that, nowadays, you don't have to think about it at all, do you?

You also washed, brushed your teeth, got dressed, ate – all without any thought involved.

In short, there are things we do every day without thinking about how to do them – we have programs we run for each of these tasks.

to succeed... JUST LET GO

On top of the basics, we do many other tasks each day without thinking about how to do them – we just do them. For example, most of us go to our place of work, at much the same time and in much the same way, every working day. If we drive, we don't need to think, as we did when we took our first driving lesson, about how to operate the car. We generally drive on "auto-pilot" and we don't think about the route we'll take to get to work – we generally follow the same program each day, only varying it should the traffic dictate and, even then, we react without a vast amount of considered thought. If we take the train or the bus to work – well, you only have to look around you, on your bus or train, at the barely alive bodies making the journey with you – again, with no thought involved.

The Value of Thought

So, even at this point, you should question the value of thought. Much of our daily existence takes place in a robot-like state of thoughtlessness. And if we did stop to think – for example, about how it is we actually walk, or drive – consider the havoc it would cause. If we stopped to consider brushing our teeth in a differenmanner – or had to re-learn how to brush our teeth each day, using our conscious mind – the routine of our day would be destroyed.
So, before we go any further – question 1: what is the value of thought?

Automatic Reactions

So far, we've considered actual useful actions which are good for us – and for which we have in-built programs so that, each time we need to execute one of those tasks, it's simply done for us.

However, many of the other things we do each day are done, yet again, without the intervention of our conscious mind. Consider the following examples.

John is one of the nicest, most easy-going people you could meet. After a relaxing breakfast one morning he offered to drive me to

You're a Robot

my next meeting. As we drove out of the hotel car park, another car pulled up in traffic blocking our way. John's reaction was immediate and completely unprintable! Within the next five minutes, he had practically rammed a couple of slow drivers, had seriously questioned the parentage of a driver who attempted to pull out into the traffic in front of us, had what seemed like deliberately tried to run down a couple of pedestrians who apparently had no right to be on a pedestrian crossing and had cursed every cyclist we passed. I haven't mentioned his reactions to buses or, interestingly enough, people driving bigger cars than his. And, also interestingly enough, John has said to me on numerous occasions over the years that he gets so stressed out by the traffic that he's a nervous wreck by the time he reaches the office – to start work – each day!

Are these the actions of a sane man, of an individual in control of his mind? Or are they reactions – something he does without thinking about it.

Or consider Dave, a highly capable person with a long-established reputation in his work. Dave recently talked to me about the stress he was suffering from at work, saying, "I am in charge of a sales force of sixty people. So, I've sixty bosses. I come in each morning. I get in about seven thirty, I've driven in from the suburbs and by the time I get to the office I'm already stressed out. I go in and I sit down in my office and I look at the list of things that I have to do this morning and I look down the list and I say to myself, 'Which will I do first?' And I know, for sure, that I'll never get half the things done that I need to do today. I sit there and I break out in cold sweat."

By the time Dave has decided on which item on his list he will do, the phone has rung and somebody has said to him "I need it this morning", and suddenly things are in an even worse mess. So by the time it gets to seven o'clock in the evening he says: "I'm there at seven o'clock in the evening trying to make up for the fact that I was disturbed so many times during the day and got nothing done. The list of things that I will look at tomorrow morning is bigger than the list that I looked at this morning. I'm in a state of total panic. I get home late and when I get in the door I start screaming at the kids!" Is this a healthy state of mind? Who, in their right mind, would

to succeed... JUST LET GO

logically decide to panic each morning? And who would decide, if they thought about it, to scream at the children they claim to love?

If Dave actually sat down and thought logically about how he reacts every morning, when he "looks forward" to the day ahead, would he decide to have that reaction? No way! Given a choice, he wouldn't place himself under that kind of pressure.

Programmed Reactions

The key question is: who in their right mind would behave like either John or Dave? And yet we're all subject to these snap reactions; if we considered how best to react in each given situation, we wouldn't knee-jerk react that way – we would act more effectively.

The fact is – a fact well established by many years of research – that, just like the programs that enable us walk, eat, drive, without thinking about it, we have programs that enable us react in given situations. These programs, like all the other programs, are "run" in our subconscious mind and we appear to have no control over them – they just happen. And, consider this – these programs, which enable us to react, often disable us from acting effectively in each given situation.

And, even more importantly as we'll see later on, these programs actually absorb, dissipate and waste our energy.

So far, we've considered reactions to external situations – like John and the traffic and Dave and his mountain of work. But what about our reactions to some of our own internal thoughts?

Another example. Peter is the National Sales Director of a large financial institution. Naturally, an important part of his job is to motivate his sales people and ensure that his management colleagues are kept abreast of how things are going and what's planned for the coming months or year. Regularly, this requires that Peter stand up, often in front of large groups, to make a presentation. Peter has been doing this for years – yet, Peter doesn't like "public speaking" (and there are many like him!). No matter how often Peter tells himself that he is going to make a slick suave presentation, when he actually stands up to speak, he fumbles, he reads from his notes, or from the slides he has prepared on the screen, and, at best, "muddles through" yet another ordeal.

If Peter were to logically think about this behaviour, would he sabotage himself? Yet he does it every time – and, try as he might, it's something that he appears not to be able to help. The sheer fact of standing up facing his audience triggers a reaction that causes all the logical and psychological arguments he has used to convince himself otherwise in advance to evaporate – his reaction to the situation is automatic!

And what about the blonde or brunette standing at the bar – simply waiting there for you to approach her – or him! How many of us really, really want to saunter nonchalantly up to that person and casually deliver just the appropriate words that will change our lives – or at least make it a night to remember! And how often does some in-built perceived inadequacy stop us? After all, if we really fancied a night (or life) to remember, logic would strongly suggest that we simply "go for it" – but how difficult it can be to think about doing it and actually do it! What is it that stops us in our tracks and creates that barrier to just doing it? And why, in each similar situation, is the reaction automatic?

Reacting to Other People

We also have automatic reactions to other people. How often have you taken and instant like or dislike to somebody – without knowing anything about them? How often do you feel drained – literally physically drained – having spent half-an-hour chatting to a particular individual? How often are you exhilarated in the presence of someone else?

In the course of a long conversation with my friend, Pat, recently, he mentioned that his girlfriend was travelling to spend a long weekend with him. On questioning he not only confessed that he wasn't looking forward to the weekend ("I find the relationship hard work at the moment") but that, after a couple of hours with her,

to succeed... JUST LET GO

he felt exhausted. And he actually claimed to be in love with this person! (Worse, we often end up marrying people like this – with all the wonderful consequences – especially for the divorce lawyers!)

I sat chatting to a client, Alan, in his office one afternoon. He was casual and relaxed. The phone rang – his body language changed, he tensed up, he spoke in clipped words. On hanging up, he spat out the words "I hate that ass-hole" – his boss! And I bet his boss knew that Alan hated him. And where did that get Alan? Eventually fired! Consider the logic of reacting like that to anyone who you believe might have any influence over any part of your life – boss, wife, husband, girlfriend, boyfriend, schoolmate – and you'll find that there is no logic.

We react to some people one way – and to others differently. We can't help it, it just happens. It's automatic – like all the other reactions that we've considered so far. Like all the other "programs" over which we have apparently little or no control!

The Power of Your Subconscious Mind

So, what's going on? Your automatic reactions are not generated from your logical, thoughtful, conscious mind. They are much deeper down – they are directly produced by your subconscious mind; from the program that keeps your heart beating as you sleep, to your automatic reaction to another person, from your ability to walk, to the panic some of us experience when we've to make a speech or handle the burden of a day's work. Your logical, thoughtful, conscious mind is helpless when it comes to controlling your automatic reactions – otherwise, we wouldn't react in the illogical fashion that prevents us achieving or doing the things we most want or need to do.

The submerged part of your very own personal iceberg runs its programs, on your behalf, and that's that! Or, at least, on the face of it, that's that! If that's where it started and ended, this book would finish here – and you'd be not only a little annoyed at having wasted your money, but having wasted it to find out something about which you can do nothing!

You're a Robot

But, of course, there's plenty we can do – or undo – to gain control of our mind (rather than the other way around) – but we had to start with a logical explanation of the first part of the basics, because we've all been trained in the dubious art of logic.

Read on!

Chapter Summary

- Your mental capacity is composed of your conscious, thinking mind and your subconscious mind.

- Your subconscious mind constantly runs a serious of "programs":

    - Your "operating programs", which enable you to function – breath, digest etc.

    - Learned programs that you use daily – walking, driving, dressing, etc. – that are useful to your daily existence

    - Behavioural programs that enable you react to situations and people – some of which are useful and some of which may not be so useful.

- Conscious, logical thought does not appear to influence your subconscious mind's ability to run these programs.

- In essence, your subconscious mind is running the show – at least inasmuch as we've explored matters so far!

Chapter Two
Your Reality

You're Not You

When you looked in the mirror this morning, to put your make-up on, or shave, who did you see? Were you entirely happy with the person in the mirror? If not, why not?

If, like most people, there's something about yourself you don't like, here's an important question. Who's doing the disliking and who's being disliked? As one of my current clients put it, for the two years during which he kept putting off doing my workshop, he was thinking, "If I discover that I'm not who I think I am, I'm afraid to discover who I might be."

Personality

The word personality is derived form the Latin "persona", meaning a mask. We all wear masks – we've a mask for the boss at work, one for the lads' or girls' night out, one for the mates at work – we react differently in each of these situations. And, like all the other reactions that we've already considered, we do this without thinking about it – we do it automatically.

But when we close our front door in the evening, with whom do we go home? Sad as it may seem, many of us also have a mask which we wear for our husband, wife or partner. But, most of all, leaving everyone and everything else aside, who do you think you are?

to succeed... JUST LET GO

You know what you're good at. You know what you can and cannot achieve. You know how far your capabilities will stretch and where your limitations lie. You know what's probable, possible and impossible. You know what's true and false, right and wrong.

At fifty years of age, George lost his job as chairman of a large financial company. He summed his predicament up like this: "I'm at a crossroads and I don't know what to do. I don't know whether I want another job in a large organisation. I don't know whether I want to work for myself. But, I'm sure of this – I'm a great sales manager, great at motivating people. I also know that if you ask me to analyse this month's management accounts, I'll freeze, because I'm stupid when it comes to figures."

I asked George who had told him that he couldn't handle figures. He answered, "No-one told me I was stupid. Some of us are born with some talents and some of us are born without others. That's the way it is." However, having reflected on my question a little more, the answer became clear – he could actually see it clearly in his mind.

He was eight years old, sitting at home in the kitchen, doing his homework – long multiplication! He was sitting there sweating, under the gaze of his father pacing up and down, pipe in mouth. His father swung around, stared him in the face and shouted: "What are you doing? Why is that taking you so long? Are you f*****g stupid?" Every night, for all his childhood, his father told him that he was "f*****g stupid". And, if you tell a child that he's stupid every night, that child will grow up believing that he is stupid!

I worked with another client, Sam, a very impressive chief executive. Sam protested: "I can't buy this child programming crap – I had a very happy childhood – I don't really remember it – I just remember it was great."

But, Sam carried the weight of the world on his shoulders, something I continued to question him about. Eventually, he replied, "I do have a memory of my childhood. I remember I was six, being driven away from my house to boarding school. And I couldn't understand why I was being sent to boarding school, I only lived forty minutes away! I remember standing beside a priest, looking at the car driving away, saying to myself: 'Why are they doing this to me?'"

Your Reality

He continued: "I have another memory, my first Communion day. I was standing in the school yard and everybody else's parents had arrived and mine were late. And I was left there on my own, wondering: 'Do they really give a damn about me at all?'"

Self-confidence – the Myth

In my own case, I have no problem believing that I'm super-intelligent – I was always told I was as a child! But, put me on a rugby pitch, or a soccer pitch or a tennis court – watch my self-confidence crumble. As a child I was told, that I had "spindly little legs" and that I was only a "small little person" and that I should "mind myself when I went out to play rough games". On many occasions, I wasn't let out to play "rough games" at all!

And what would my father tell me, before I would go out to play tennis? "I don't know why you bother, you always lose." And, of course, he was right!

Most of us have an inferiority complex about something about ourselves I'm not saying that we're all going around feeling inferior all the time, although some people are. What I'm saying is that most people have an inferiority complex about something. Where do we get these ideas from – and why would we sabotage ourselves or feel inadequate? The world's a rough enough place without our having to fight ourselves too!

The fact is that your personality was formed when you were a child – that's why those years are called your formative years! This mask – who you think you are – is a set of completely automatic programs. Like all the programs we've considered, this mask is run from your subconscious mind – so you're not even conscious that you think you are this person, you just believe it to be true.

And, even though most of us were brought up in a very loving environment, with the best of intentions parents, automatically driven by their own programming, start limiting our potential. Consider the throw-away remarks that we as parents, make to our children. For example, a child might say, "I'm going to build a spaceship!" or

to succeed... JUST LET GO

"When I get bigger I'm going to be a movie star", and you just throw away the remark, "Ah, that's ridiculous", or "Don't be stupid".

These little things with which we constantly pepper our children actually seep into their subconscious – if they hear it often enough they believe it of themselves. We do little things to our children all the time that have a massive impact on their view of the world and most importantly on their view of themselves. These events, little or large to the adult mind, can create the most life-changing pictures or programs in the child's mind.

Adrian told me that he had never heard his father sing in his entire life! Even at three in the morning when everybody was pissed, his father would stay steadfastly silent throughout the sing-song.

Then, after many years of wondering about this, Adrian was at a family get-together last Christmas and, late at night, the Christmas carols started. As always, his father sat in the corner, like a statue. Adrian said to his grandaunt, "I've never heard my father singing." She said, "Oh, I remember the last time he sang. It was at a party about seventy years ago! He was only four or five at the time. When he got up to sing everybody broke their hearts laughing and he's never opened his mouth since!"

Your Family Album

Ever heard the expression "young and impressionable"? Well, that's how we all were as children. Anything that happened to you, that was big enough to grab your attention, went straight into your subconscious mind as a picture, as if you had taken a photograph – it's what psychologists call snapshot learning.

As you grew up you were told what is true and false, right and wrong. So, by the time you reached eleven or twelve years of age, you knew what is true in the world and what is not true, what you're capable of and you knew what you're not capable of! All these pictures or programs that you have, actually form your picture of what you can and cannot do. The perspective you have of what you can achieve is someone else's. And, regardless of how well you were

Your Reality

brought up, this view falls far short of your true, unlimited potential. Your own unique photograph album, composed of all the things people did to or for you and the events that created an impression on your mind, is your point of reference for who you think you are and what you think you're capable of. These are the photographs you will refer back to for the rest of your life.

On top of your Operating System (breathing, digesting, etc) and your Action Programs (walking, driving, etc.) and on top of your Reaction Programs (panic, calm, etc.) there is another layer of programs that gives you your view of who you are. This, you call, your Personality – and it's totally a figment of your imagination!

Actually, it's even worse than that. As you've seen, your personality is actually a figment of someone else's imagination. You are the product of your upbringing, your surroundings and your society.

Society is Not on Your Side

Along with the specific personality traits that you possess, we all have a general predisposition to greatly underestimate our true potential. All our surroundings conspire against us – almost from the word go. Picture it – it's three o'clock in the morning, your three-month-old baby has been crying non-stop for hours. Most parents will not openly admit to shouting at their children, but, at the same time, I don't know a parent who has not shouted at an infant at some stage. The message the infant gets is, "I get into trouble for crying – even if I've a very good reason to cry. I shouldn't try to please myself. I should try to conform to what other people want of me."

After a few months, your baby begins to crawl – all the way into the fire! Rather than calmly saying, "Darling, don't put your hand in the fire, you'll burn yourself," your instinctive reaction is to scream at him and drag him away. He was only exploring! But, the message he gets has, once again, a double meaning. "Fires are dangerous." He might get that message after four or five attempts! But, he also gets what is, by now, becoming a fairly familiar message. "I shouldn't do what I want to do. I should do what someone else wants me to

to succeed... JUST LET GO

do." Then he starts walking, and he tries to pull the kettle down on himself. The same double message is repeated – one helpful, the other, which he keeps on hearing – "Don't do what you want to do, do what someone else wants you to do."

Then, he goes to school, and he's told to "Stand in line", "Sit up straight", "Pay attention", "Stop making noise" – all the things a little kid doesn't want to do! There's that message again, "Don't do what you want to do, do what someone else wants you to do" – conform. When he's six or seven, he starts learning about God – and God's will is largely defined by a set of rules that dictate what he shouldn't do! Then he has his first relationship. And if things are really going well, she will tell him, "I love you". But no-one ever just says "I love you". What people always really say is "I love you, if"! That's not what they actually say, but that's what they actually mean. "I love you if you please me", "I love you if you do what I want you to do", "I love you subject to these terms and conditions", "I love you because you love me".

There is a constant theme running through our formative years. We shouldn't do what we want to do ourselves. We should conform to what other people expect of us, what God expects of us, what society expects of us. This is a constant underlying subliminal message reinforcing the boundaries beyond which you cannot go as a person. As a result, we end up living a life that we were told to live, living within parameters beyond which we know we cannot go, wearing a bodysuit that has been manufactured for us – our personality, who we think we are.

Your Virtual Reality

By the time you're a teenager, you know what's possible and impossible, what's right and wrong, who you are and who you're not. After that, just like all the other programs we discussed in Chapter 1, everything happens automatically. You want to talk to that girl at the bar – something tells you that you can't; you want to impress your management colleagues at the meeting on the annual accounts – but you know you're stupid; you know what I'm talking about.

Your Reality

These things happen, without you giving them active logical thought – because, if you did, you could simply decide, "No, I'm not stupid", "I'm not shy", "I'm not awkward", "I'm not a loser". But you cannot simply decide – because all these automatic "knowings" come from your subconscious mind.

Your reality is not my reality. Even for two intimate people sharing the same experience, each person's "reality" represents their own view of that experience, based on their view of the world. Consider the implications of that from the perspective of managing family relationships or a so-called management team. Just picture it; you've five or six people sitting in the same room, living in parallel universes!

Every person has their own peculiar and particular view of "reality" – and your "reality" is the result of the programs that you are running, at this moment in time, to actually create your "reality".

This shouldn't come as news to you! Firstly, the conditioning or programs that we took on board when we were young forms our view of who we are and the world we live in. Now these programs are running in your subconscious mind, and you're totally unaware that it's happening. But, that's not to say that it's not actually happening!

Regardless of whether or not you are aware of this, this is how your mind works. Your subconscious mind dictates whether you react to a particular person by snapping at them or by being warm to them. Your subconscious mind determines how you react to pressure, to that certain phone call, how you react to other people, how you "feel" today, whether you're in good form or "depressed", whether you believe you can cope or succeed, whether you see yourself achieving or failing.

In short, your subconscious mind runs the whole show – and it runs that show based on the programs you're running. It's rather like a PlayStation or virtual reality computer game – except you don't have the controls! The game's CD is made up of all the pictures you "snapped" in your formative years that show you what your life is like and how to behave in each situation that this "life" throws at you. Like all computer games, you can't go outside the game and you must play by the rules.

to succeed... JUST LET GO

And we'd all be doomed if we couldn't change the CD! But, if you understand the mechanics of how your virtual reality is produced, then you're equipped to actually take the controls and create the virtual reality that you really, really want.

Chapter Summary

- Your personality is a mask created by your subconscious mind.

- The programs that create who you think you are were given to you during your formative years – as a child.

- The expectation of others and of society means that, even with the best of upbringings, we all believe ourselves to be considerably less than we really can be.

- Your programs create your personality and your reality. They are "run" in your subconscious mind – conscious, logical thought is powerless to override them.

Chapter Three
The Mechanics of Your Mind

Your Beliefs

It should not come as a shock to you, that your beliefs are simply a set of pictures or programs stored safely, beyond the reach of logical thought, in your subconscious mind.

We learn our beliefs as children and our subconscious mind stores them as pictures. Some of these pictures are built up through an ongoing regular process of experience – like George who was told he was stupid every night. Some pictures are snapped, just like a photograph. This happens when your attention is grabbed by a big enough event.

One sunny Sunday afternoon, my daughter, Louise, toddled out into our front garden – she was about two years old at the time. As she marched in her own inimitable style over to our garden gate, a little white puppy charged across the field in front of our house – to play with her. He bounded into our garden, jumped up on her, placing his front paws on her chest – and frightened the living daylights out of her. Quite literally, the puppy grabbed all of Louise's attention. For many years afterwards, Louise demanded to be carried in our arms if there was a dog within a hundred yards! That's snapshot learning.

Something that is big enough to grab all of your attention directly accesses your subconscious mind, your subconscious mind takes a photograph – it's that simple.

to succeed... JUST LET GO

When Experiencing Stops

Once you've collected your very own personal album of pictures, generally speaking, you stop experiencing life and start existing – I'm loath to use the word living, because most people are not – by reference to your pictures. You see the world, and your place in it, through your preconceived notions of what you think is happening and what you think is real. For every situation, every moment, every day, your subconscious mind has a reference point which enables you to understand what's happening and you react accordingly. But you do your understanding according to your set of pictures and you react according to those pictures – not to what's really happening but what your subconscious mind, running its programs, imagines is happening. You don't actually experience what's really happening, you react to what you imagine is happening, by reliving an experience which made an impression on you as a child.

Let's understand how this actually works. Pat had a big problem with public speaking. Every time he stood up in front of a group of people he froze. But what was actually happening was that he had stood up in front of his classmates when he was seven years old, in the month of May, which is significant because he'd just got into short trousers, and his classmates started to laugh at his legs! Now, every time he stands up to make a speech in front of a group of people, his subconscious mind pulls up the original picture of a group of guys laughing at him and this triggers his reaction.

Without going into all the gory details, Carl had major difficulties with relationships – he tried to control his girlfriend, Anne, to prove to himself that she loved him. One night, returning from a girls' night out, Anne noticed that she was being followed by a car, all the way into her apartment building car park – it was Carl, who claimed he just happened to be passing but who admitted to me that he was checking to see that Anne wasn't out with someone else. After they'd been going out together a few months, Anne gave Carl a key to her apartment only to wake up in the middle of one night to find Carl standing at the end of her bed, at four o'clock in the morning – again he was checking up on her. Carl's problem

The Mechanics of Your Mind

was that he didn't believe anyone could love him. Carl had a very clear picture of himself when he was eleven years old standing in the kitchen with his mum standing at the sink and his dad leaning against the heater. Carl had put on a massive spurt of growth, virtually overnight, and his new school coat resembled a short-sleeved jacket! His mother was demanding that his father give her money to buy him a new coat – and his father was screaming that he'd only bought him a coat a couple of months ago. In the end, under much pressure, Carl's father swore at him, took a ten shilling note from his wallet and threw the money at Carl. Carl says that the whole thing appeared to happen in dramatic slow motion – all three watched as the note hit Carl on the chest and gently dropped to the floor. Carl remembers saying to himself "Is that all I'm worth?" The result – Carl now needs to prove to himself that someone he loves loves him. Every time he gets close to someone, his subconscious runs the "ten shilling note film" and he starts behaving in a way that he admits to be totally irrational – but he cannot seem to stop it; he cannot seem to control himself.

I really want to labour this point – it is so important to appreciate that you're not living what is real, you're not experiencing what is real, you're experiencing what you imagine is real, based on your virtual reality, based on your pictures, in your subconscious mind.

How can two people have exactly the same experience and one be delighted whilst the other might be absolutely distraught? It has nothing to do with what actually happened, it has to do with each person's attitude to what they imagine happened and, consequently, what they believed themselves to have experienced. Of course, neither of them actually experienced what happened, they both replayed some old movie from their album!

You Ignore What You Don't Believe is True

Once you've established your set of beliefs, you filter out what doesn't fit with your beliefs. For example, many people have a problem taking a compliment or accepting praise, because it doesn't fit with

to succeed... JUST LET GO

their view of who they are. Dermot was a very shy, self-conscious person, whose job was training insurance brokers. He travelled the country and was a terrific public speaker – he put on a performance or mask that wasn't him. Invariably, people would come up to him after a presentation and say, "Wow, that was brilliant." But, each time, Dermot felt very uneasy and would immediately change the subject; praise didn't fit with his feelings of inferiority and so he'd brush the comments aside. In doing so, he actually didn't really hear the comments at all.

On a deeper level, try telling a Muslim extremist that, when he dies, he'll most probably sit alongside a Jew beyond the pearly gates! Try telling a Christian fundamentalist that other Christians are just as likely to be saved as he is.

Changing Your Beliefs

Because your beliefs are stored in your subconscious, a contrary view put forward by reasoned argument, using logical thought, will be rejected out of hand – your conscious mind cannot change your beliefs. Why was it that scientists were burned for claiming the world isn't flat or that the sun doesn't go around the earth? The production of clear evidence to the contrary, such as the constant accolades heaped on Dermot for his presentations – all his listeners couldn't be wrong – makes no difference. Your beliefs, once held (or photographed), cannot be altered, unless you can gain access to your subconscious mind. And yet, your beliefs are no more than programs!

The Normal Person's Reality

The millions of years' programming you were born with, together with an average education and a couple of normal parents, will provide the normal person with a view of their world that "life is not too bad", "you take the rough with the smooth", you ride the rollercoaster of "life's little ups and downs", you get an education,

The Mechanics of Your Mind

get a job, earn a living, etc., etc. Indeed, some world religions would have the normal person believe that "I'm a hopeless sinner struggling to get somewhere better when I die" – and if you're happy or wealthy in the meantime, well, tough, you've had your reward.

And so we live according to the programs that were given us, we pass those programs on to our own children and those over whom we have any influence, and life becomes a long string of self-fulfilling prophecies which are, in general, not too bad!

University research indicates that 96 per cent of people live this way – 96 per cent of people are *normal*. But, if you consider that it's your subconscious mind that runs the whole show, you'll discover that normal people are mad – their mind controls them, not the other way around. To put it a little more bluntly, normal people have lost their minds.

Your Beliefs Can Overcome the Impossible

Enough of normal people for a moment. In many well-documented cases, the subconscious PlayStation can create spectacular results.

Twenty seventy year olds were selected at random from a number of retirement-homes and placed in a controlled environment, under university research conditions, where their surroundings were designed to help them believe that they were, in fact, living in the early 1960s. The cars parked outside were of the period, news bulletins and music from 1961 or 1962 were on the radio and the newspapers and magazines provided for them were of the same vintage. The clothes they wore were from the early 1960s and the food they were eating was early 1960s. These conditions were provided for seven days.

During those seven days, some who had used reading glasses stopped using them. One person, who had been unable to walk without the aid of a Zimmer-frame, was able to walk unassisted and a couple of participants started jogging each morning. Most notable of all – in the case of twelve individuals, their fingers (not finger-nails) had grown longer. What your mind believes can make a fundamental difference to your health and well-being.

to succeed... JUST LET GO

During one of my workshops, I was discussing this when I was stopped, in my tracks, by a girl. She said to me, "My father was diagnosed with cancer eight years ago – told he had three months to live. But Dad said to me, 'There is no way that I am not living to walk you down the aisle' – I was seventeen at the time! Last summer, I got married and Dad 'gave me away' and he made his 'Father-of-the-Bride' speech. At the end of the evening, he died." His goal had been achieved.

The Chinese have an expression, "We grow old because we see those around us grow old". It intrigues me how accurate doctors are when they say to cancer patients, "You've three months to live", "You've six months to live", "You've twelve months to live". Is it the cancer that kills the patient after the three, six or twelve months? Or is an announcement, such as that, from an authoritative figure to a vulnerable patient, enough to grab the patient's attention so that their subconscious mind photographs the event meaning it becomes one of their self-fulfilling beliefs?

Within you, you have the ability to be one of the 4 per cent – to achieve virtually unlimited success. You do not need to add anything to yourself, to learn from anyone else, all you need is within you, as you are right now – but, and this is an important 'but', not as you think you are right now. All you have to do is grasp the ability within. You grasp it by taking control of your subconscious mind and not living the way the 96 per cent lives, where the subconscious mind has control of them.

Clarity of Mind

Understanding that your subconscious takes its photographs, which form your reality, when it is totally focused, provides you with your first clue to the clarity of mind you'll require to change your reality to what you really, really want. Young children experience this clarity of mind all of the time. That's how a seven-year-old boy can charge out of the cinema believing he's Superman or Frodo Baggins!

The Mechanics of Your Mind

Have you ever sat through a three-hour film that totally grabbed your attention and thought that you had only been sitting there twenty minutes? When you are so totally focused on what you're doing "time flies". When you're in that state of mind, you are experiencing the clarity of mind that children are in all the time. This clarity of mind is the key to accessing your subconscious mind and harnessing your unlimited power and potential.

As an adult, you experience this clarity of mind from time to time; for example, if you're a golfer, when you stand up on the tee and swing, and you hit the most wonderful drive, so wonderful it feels like you didn't hit the ball at all – it was effortless. You're just there in the moment, and you say to yourself "How did I do that?" And would you be able to do it again? Of course, when you try to do it from the next tee, the ball goes off around the corner – sometimes never to be seen again! And the reason it goes off around the corner is you're trying too hard.

Have you ever gone out for the evening at eight o'clock and suddenly realised it's three o'clock in the morning and you wonder, "Where did the last seven hours go?" You're just there, in the moment, without thoughts, worries or concerns – you're just having a good time! When you're in this clarity of mind you have actually accessed your subconscious mind, you are in that state of mind in which your subconscious mind takes its pictures.

The problem with most people is, not only can they not access their subconscious minds, they don't even know that their subconscious minds are there to be accessed! By its very definition, you're not conscious of your subconscious mind. In addition, your subconscious is guarded against intruders – by what psychologists call the sentry – so that others cannot access your subconscious, otherwise they could then brainwash you. Unfortunately, however, the sentry also ensures that you cannot get past either! However, there are ways to free your mind from the incessant noise of useless thought that preoccupies us daily and, in the process, by-pass the sentry.

to succeed... JUST LET GO

Freeing Your Mind

Over the millennia, mystics of all traditions have spoken about clarity of mind. As a result, many forms of meditation are designed to move us towards this clear state of being. However, early last century, science – something that many logical minds take comfort from! – began to tie down the nature of this clarity of mind. Consequently, we now largely understand how to consciously invoke clarity of mind within each of us.

Our story begins with Thomas Edison, the man who gave us all-day daylight, among four hundred other patented inventions. Like most of us, Edison did his work during the day – and during an average day, like all of us, he might encounter problems or have new ideas. However, he noticed that it was at night, as he fell asleep, that the solution to a problem would come to him effortlessly – or a new idea would just drift into his consciousness. So, as a first step, he placed a notepad beside his bed – when something "popped into his head", he could write or draw it in his notebook. Eventually, he said to himself: "Why should I wait until eleven o'clock at night to invent? Why should I wait until I drift into this 'twilight zone' to get these ideas? Why should I leave it to chance, where I might get the solution to my problem late at night and be too tired to write it down, and it would be gone again the following morning?"

He decided to set about consciously bringing about that clear state of mind when he decided, rather than waiting for it to happen, and developed a number of exercises to get himself into that state of mind whenever he decided. Edison was well known for requiring little sleep each night, so it was with great suprise, when Henry Ford called on Edison in the middle of the afternoon and asked his assistant, "Can I see the great man?" he learned that "The great man is taking a nap!" To the uninitiated observer, he was indeed taking a nap, but we now know that he was actually relaxing into that deep state of clarity of mind.

Indeed, there have been many well-known "nappers" over the centuries, some of the best known include Napoleon Boneparte, Leonardo da Vinci and Winston Churchill, who spent half the day

The Mechanics of Your Mind

in bed! Nowadays, many top business people, top-performing sports-people and athletes take the same approach. The only thing that they all have in common is that they are exceptionally successful – they're not members of the 96 per cent club!

These top performers have been using the power of their subconscious mind in a very structured way, doing it deliberately, rather than leaving it to chance. As a result, university research within the last forty years has been devoted to exploring the nature of this clarity of mind and its significance in relation to how we achieve, succeed and live our lives.

Science Validates Mysticism

Around the same time that scientific research began to explore the last great unexplored frontier – the inner you – people like the great spiritualist and mystic, Anthony deMello, were explaining how you can bring about that clarity of mind. DeMello, an Indian Jesuit priest, fused age-old Eastern mysticism with Western religion and culture and put forward ancient meditative techniques remarkably similar to the exercises being examined and validated by bastions of Western science such as the universities of Chicago and Harvard.

Scientific research across the globe was focusing on what the University of Chicago has defined as The Flow – what top sports-people would define as being in the zone, what people like American psychologist Jerry Kushel define as the peak performance zone. Western science has now validated that there is indeed a clear state of mind in which you perform better and which you can use to set your mind to achieve results beyond the reasonable norm. It is also now accepted that you can bring about this clarity of mind yourself and that the more you do it, the more effective you become and the greater and more effortless will be the results.

This clarity of mind is the state of mind we discussed at the beginning of this chapter, which only comes to normal people in fleeting moments and, consequently, is of no practical use to them.

to succeed... JUST LET GO

A Clear Mind is the Key to Success

Clarity of mind is the key to re-setting your belief in what you can achieve, because it is the state of mind in which you snapped those pictures that formed the programs that created your personality and now run your virtual reality computer game. If you can get back to that state of mind, get into where your programs are stored, you can change your view of the world and change your life – or, maybe, start living – and we now have the proven means to do it. That is the significance of clarity of mind – it is the key to living life to the full, it is the key to achieving all your goals, it is the key to exceptional success.

Chapter Summary

- Your beliefs are stored in your subconscious as pictures taken as a child.

- You took your pictures when all of your mind was focused – either through snapshot learning or through constant, regular experience.

- You stop experiencing as an adult – your pictures are the programs you repeatedly run as an adult. They trigger your reactions and behaviour, based on old experiences.

- Conscious, logical thought cannot change your beliefs – they can only be changed in your subconscious mind.

- You access your subconscious by clearing your mind, using time-honoured and validated techniques.

- This clarity of mind is the sole key to achieving your dreams and goals.

PART TWO

Switching Yourself On

Chapter Four
Free Your Mind

Your Subconscious Rules OK!

Regardless of how much you want to achieve something, if your subconscious mind says no, the answer is no! Some years ago, at a major international banking conference in Barcelona, I went into the Gents before sitting down to hear the main speaker, who was in the toilet, pacing up and down, psyching himself up before his presentation. It was like visiting a prize fighter in his dressing-room just before a world-title bout! With great fanfare, he approached the stage – and read from his handout, droning on for an hour and putting most of the audience to sleep. All his pre-speech effort was futile, because he was trying to convince himself in his conscious mind. If you set yourself a goal that you don't believe you can achieve, your chances of success are nil, they're not 50:50 – you either believe you can do it or you can't do it at all.

There are a lot of motivational speakers and writers who tell you that you should leap out of bed in the morning, look in the mirror and say, "Oh! This is a wonderful day, this is the best day of my life," or, "I'm great, I'm wonderful, I'm a great person, I really look fabulous, I am fabulous." Doing this is like throwing mud, some of it might eventually stick, because you're trying to convince your conscious mind and your conscious mind is not an awful lot of use to you!

to succeed... JUST LET GO

Your subconscious mind brings about whatever it is that you set your subconscious mind to create – whether you know or understand this is beside the point, this is how your mind creates your "reality" anyway. So, if your life is "not too bad", you have that "not too bad" life because you set your subconscious mind to give you that kind of life – all completely subconsciously, of course! To live an abnormal life, a life beyond the "not too bad", you've got to change your subconscious mind – that is the task before you.

Clarity of Mind

You change your subconscious mind when you're experiencing the clarity of mind that makes time fly – the clarity of mind that children are in all the time and in which you subconsciously acquired your original programs. As you already know, from when your mind has been that clear – for example, that perfect golf shot, the film that "captured your imagination", that night out when seven hours seemed like thirty minutes, that day before your holidays when you got a month's work done by lunchtime! – this clarity is an experience of being relaxed, just doing what you're doing, of being there, achieving, not thinking about what you're doing, not worrying, your mind not wandering, a feeling of being so focused that you're not even aware that you're focused.

To change your subconscious mind – so that it can quite literally give you what you really want – to change your beliefs and your view of yourself and of the world, to change your perception of what is and isn't possible, you need to become proficient at experiencing that clarity of mind – when you decide, as distinct from when it simply happens to you.

Stopping the Traffic

Normally, when you're going about your so-called normal day, your mind isn't clear, it's clogged with a lot of useless thought, it

Free Your Mind

wanders – apparently of its own free will! – it encourages you to think before you do, when you know that just doing is much more efficient and effective. You are constantly distracted.

Research indicates that, each day, some tens of thousands of random thoughts enter our conscious mind. Some are useful, most are not. For example, how many times have you been doing something when it occurs to you that you should remember to do something else – something else you can't remember afterwards? How often do great ideas come to you in the middle of something else that you're supposed to be doing and nothing comes of that idea? How many of us half do our job each day thinking that we'd like to be somewhere else – when the only place we can actually be is where we are? And how many people spend their day at work thinking about how unfair the system is, that someone else got promoted when they really deserved it? To take this to the extreme, consider the story of Keith and Colin – both managers in an insurance company. Colin's office was newly painted, whilst Keith's wasn't. Not only did Keith waste days on end agonising over how unfair life was, the company's General Manager wasted days trying to get the painter back to do Keith's office!

The fact is that normal people's minds are distracted and wandering all of the time – and it's pretty difficult to be successful if your mind is somewhere else! Therefore, the first step towards clarity of mind is to stop all this incessant, useless traffic that's clogging up your freeway. To do this, you need to calm down and relax – yes, it is that simple (and that difficult!).

Relaxation – Traffic-calming Measures!

The first thing you need to learn is how to relax. Many of my clients give me a strange look when I first mention this – but the fact is that few of us know how to really relax or are even comfortable with the concept of doing nothing, even if it's only for a couple of minutes. However, the first thing that practising deep relaxation achieves is that it stops the traffic, enabling you to begin to understand and experience the

to succeed... JUST LET GO

difference between your normal fragmented mind and an abnormal calm, clear mind.

The exercises my clients use are not normal – and that is most people's initial reaction to any of the exercises in this chapter! Dead right, they're not normal. Normal people don't do them – highly successful people do them. A number of people have asked me "Is this hypnosis?" or "Is this self-hypnosis?" The answer: you've been living in a hypnotic trance all of your life up to now, unwittingly hypnotised by other people's programs that you take for granted, blissfully unaware that you can achieve everything to which you set your mind, effortlessly. It's time to snap yourself out of that hypnotic trance, to stop behaving like a brainless robot, to stop existing (as distinct from living) in the twilight zone of someone else's PlayStation game.

Others have asked me "Why do I need to do any of these exercises?" The answer: simply telling a forty-year-old overweight slob that he's going to run a marathon later today won't enable him do it (it'll probably kill him!). You need to train. And most people, up to now happy to live their "not too bad" lives, are the mental equivalent of the overweight slob, smoking forty a day as well. Your mind is untrained, lazy, sluggish, distracted and slow – and you're not in control of it.

Bear in mind that the sole purpose of all the exercises in this chapter is to enable you become mentally fit – to enable you use more of your mind, to enable you to become more successful and live a better life, effortlessly. So, are you ready?

Some Ground Rules

Millennia of meditative practice indicate that the straighter your back whilst doing any of these mental exercises, the more effective your training will be. So, as a preference, you should do these exercises whilst sitting down (or sitting up!), rather than lying down. On no account should you do any of these exercises whilst driving! So, find yourself a straight-backed chair – no useful training was ever

Free Your Mind

done slouching! Alternatively, you could sit erect on the floor (but I find that more of a distraction than a help).

Secondly, don't cross your legs or fold your arms – we want your energy to flow freely, not to be blocked by such obstructions. So, if you're sitting on a chair, put your two feet firmly on the floor, and the palms of your hands on your legs.

Thirdly, find somewhere where you won't be disturbed whilst doing these exercises. I accept that, in modern life, it is improbable if not impossible that you will find somewhere that is completely silent – physical silence, in all probability doesn't exist. But it's not physical silence we're seeking, it's mental silence, a completely different commodity, which can use the sounds around you, as we'll see, to deepen that mental stillness.

Finally, none of these exercises is suggested for its own sake alone – they are all for the greater purpose of enabling you become a trained exponent of the art of achieving clarity of mind – so that you can use your clarity of mind to live your life to the full. Always bear this in mind. If you don't, these exercises become like your last diet, or joining the gym as your New Year's resolution and going twice, or giving up chocolate because you know it's bad for you! They will be nothing more than another fad that you will let fall by the wayside and which you will discount as something else that didn't work – because you didn't stick with it and put it to its intended use.

Relaxation Exercise 1 – Listening

This exercise is designed to slow your mind down, to calm your mind, clear it of thought by focusing on the sounds around you.

1. Assume the position – sitting upright, feet firmly on the floor, hands on your legs.

2. Whenever you feel comfortable, let your eyes gently close.

3. Listen and notice all of the sounds you hear.

to succeed... JUST LET GO

4. Notice that each sound becomes clearer, you can even notice the quietest of sounds.

5. If – or when – a distracting thought crosses your mind, notice it for what it is (a distraction) and return to listening to all the sounds around you.

6. Let each sound add to your feeling of comfort and relaxation.

7. Continue to refocus on each of the sounds for a number of minutes.

8. In your own good time, when you're ready, open your eyes.

Relaxation exercise 1 – summary

Sit upright – eyes close – focus on each sound – each sound relaxes you more – when distracted, focus on each sound.

Getting Fitter

The scientific world now accepts that you can, of your own accord, achieve clarity of mind. We build on our level of clarity of mind each time we do any of these exercises – we never go back to the start, once we've opened the door to our subconscious mind, it's open! But we have to keep working on it, each day you should practice whichever of the exercises in this chapter best suit you – different exercises suit different people.

Free Your Mind

Relaxation Exercise 2 – Your Body

This exercise is designed to clear your mind by focusing on the sensations in your body and by consciously relaxing different parts of your body, in random order.

1. Assume the position – sitting upright, feet firmly on the floor, hands on your legs.

2. Whenever you feel comfortable, let your eyes gently close.

3. Focus on your feet – the feeling of the floor underneath them – on each toe, one by one. Relax each toe, one by one, feeling the fresh air between each one.

4. Focus on your shoulders – notice if there's any tension in the muscles of your shoulders. Relax this area, visualising the muscles slackening, feeling any "weight of the world" being lifted from your shoulders.

5. Focus on your hands – feel how they rest on your legs – on each finger, one by one. Relax each finger, feeling the energy in your fingertips.

6. Focus on your forehead and the top of your head – notice if there's any tension in your forehead – feel your "worry lines" being smoothed away – feel your energy rise as the whole area becomes more relaxed.

7. If – or when – a distracting thought crosses your mind, notice it for what it is (a distraction) and return to an area of your body other than the one you were focusing on when distracted.

8. Repeat your focus on each body area as before – feet, shoulders, hands, head.

9. Let each feeling add to your level of comfort and relaxation.

10. In your own good time, when you're ready, open your eyes.

to succeed... JUST LET GO

Relaxation exercise 2 – summary

Sit upright – eyes close – feet and toes – shoulders – hands and fingers – forehead and top of head – each sensation relaxes you more – when distracted, go to next body area – repeat the focus on each part of your body a couple of times.

Relaxation Exercise 3 – Breathing

This exercise is put forward by many meditative exponents as the most powerful means of clearing your mind to a fantastically deep or clear level – by focusing on your breath.

1. Assume the position – sitting upright, feet firmly on the floor, hands on your legs.

2. Whenever you feel comfortable, let your eyes gently close.

3. Listen and notice the sounds of your breathing – normal breathing, not deep breaths.

4. Count your breaths, noticing each inhalation and exhalation, both of which count as one. Count from one to four then start again at one.

5. If – or when – a distracting thought crosses your mind, notice it for what it is (a distraction) and restart your counting at one.

6. Let each breath deepen your feeling of comfort and relaxation.

7. In your own good time, when you're ready, open your eyes.

Free Your Mind

Relaxation exercise 3 – summary

Sit upright – eyes close – listen to breaths – count breaths one to four and repeat.

Relaxation Exercise 4 – Your Eyes

I have found that a number of my clients favour this particular exercise – however, it doesn't suit everybody and, once again, I would emphasise that you will progress best by using the exercise or exercises that suit *you* best.

1. Assume the position – sitting upright, feet firmly on the floor, hands on your legs.

2. Whenever you feel comfortable, let your eyes gently close.

3. One at a time, focus on and relax your feet, shoulders, hands and forehead – but only once, do not repeat this.

4. Focus on your eyes – feel how relaxed the muscles around your eyes are – feel how heavy your eyelids are.

5. Notice your eyelids becoming heavier – as if there were a lead weight in the bottom of your upper eyelids.

6. When you're ready, try to open your eyes – but you will find that your eyelids are so relaxed that you are unable to open them.

7. Stop trying – and let yourself slip deeper into relaxation and let that feeling grow by simply listening to your breathing.

8. In your own good time, when you're ready, open your eyes.

to succeed... JUST LET GO

Relaxation exercise 4 – summary

Sit upright – eyes close – feet, shoulders, hands, forehead – relax your eyes – eyelids get heavier – try to open eyes, you cannot – stop trying, listen to your breathing – slip into deeper relaxation.

The Purpose of Relaxation

The exercises on the previous pages are not designed to put you to sleep – in fact, the exact opposite is the case – they are designed to clear your mind and, if anything, make you more lucid and more alert. Remember, that the sole purpose of these exercises is to begin to train your mind to take its instructions from you rather than to take its instructions from programs you have been running all of your life.

In fact, in doing these exercises, what you've done is you've let your energy come to the surface, whereas normally – and it's an appallingly stupid thing to do – you actually suppress your energy. You have this power within you which you can harness at any point in time, but you can't just say: "Right, I'm in that state of mind now." You have to train yourself – that's what these exercises are all about.

Reaction to the Exercises

People's reactions to these exercises vary, as you might expect, however there are three things everyone has in common. Firstly, when doing any of the exercises, you will feel that what really takes ten minutes only feels like one or two – as we've already said, when you're in that clear state of mind time flies! Secondly, you will feel far more relaxed than you would after a normal night's sleep – very many people don't know what a deep relaxing sleep feels like and, in fact, your subconscious is not necessarily calm whilst you sleep – after all, that's the part of your mind that dreams. Thirdly, my own research also shows that, after each of these exercises, your pulse

Free Your Mind

rate will be considerably less – by up to one-third – than your normal resting pulse rate following a relaxing night's sleep. All this indicates that, in our modern world, people don't know how to relax – and, to repeat, relaxation is not falling asleep in front of the television.

Beyond that, people's experiences or reactions to the exercises are as different as individuals are! However, there are some common reactions. For example, many people feel a tingling sensation, either in their fingers or on their forehead. This is the beginning of the bubbling up of your inner energy – who you really are inside beginning to bubble up to the surface. Some find it quite a frightening experience the first time they do any of these exercises, feeling that some other force has taken over. Of course, the force they're experiencing is their own life force that has been locked up behind the iron bars of thought and programming for all of their adult life. This is the force that is available to you to do anything you want to do, effortlessly. As Nelson Mandela has said: "Our deepest fear is not that we are inadequate. Our deepest fear is that we are powerful beyond reason. It is our light, not our darkness, that frightens us."

Indeed, another common reaction is that people actually see that light, I know I do. Some researchers in this area compare this light to the light seen by those who've had a near-death experience – I would well believe it. Again, as you're freeing up the energy within, it is only natural that many experience a different level of inner being, inner peace and inner power that sometimes shocks, always surprises – and is the real you.

Of course, if you experience none of these what does that mean? Absolutely nothing! Each of us is different. This is not a competition; your own goal must be to find that clarity of mind in you, for yourself, as it suits you – and you know what? – when you access your subconscious mind, you'll know and only you will know for sure.

Progressing

After some training – after a good few sessions in the mental gym – the object will be to be able to switch yourself into that clarity of mind at

to succeed... JUST LET GO

will. The exercises in this chapter are the foundations (the ground and first floors will be added later – read on). But you must be disciplined – toning your mental muscles takes commitment – maybe as much as fifteen minutes out of the twenty-four hours available to you each day! But the prize is great – it has been variously described over the centuries as "a pearl of great price", "Shangri-La" or "peace beyond understanding" – and that it certainly is. But it is more – putting this clarity of mind first in your life means that you become far more successful at the other things that normal people put all their energy into – like making money, "earning a living", getting a bigger job or house – if that's what turns you on.

And speaking of turning you on – these exercises are designed to do just that – turn you on. Do you realise that you've been turned off, like a television on standby, for all of your adult life up to now? Go on, turn yourself on. The more exercises you do, the more skilled you become at accessing your subconscious mind. The deeper you can get into your subconscious mind, the bigger the pictures you will be able to add to your photo album. The bigger the pictures, the more immediate the effect, because, strangely enough, your subconscious mind is like a child's mind – it'll always reference the big, glossy, colour photos first!

Your commitment to a new effortless life is no more than fifteen minutes each day – and as you progress, your natural state will move from the current "not too bad" to one of a readily clearer state of mind – so your time commitment to these exercises will diminish over time, as your new life kicks in. And all you'll leave behind are the curren distractions of worry, useless thought, the daily struggle, the treadmill, the rat-race – all the things that snatch your energy That's not a very high price to pay, is it? But – and it's entirely up to you – do put those fifteen minutes aside, very deliberately, each day. Some of my clients got into the habit of doing their exercises before they get up each morning. Eight years into my own work and research in this area, I believe that that's not good enough – you must "sit up straight" and do your chores! But more of that in Chapter 13!

Free Your Mind

Chapter Summary

- You can change nothing if you can't change your subconscious mind.

- Achieving clarity of mind is the only way into your subconscious.

- Your mind is clogged with rubbish – you need to free your mind.

- You unclog your mind – and achieve clarity of mind – by relaxing it.

- This relaxation is achieved through a disciplined approach, using a series of exercises designed for this sole purpose.

- There are rules you should observe – best practices! – to attain best results.

- Put aside fifteen minutes a day specifically for your exercises.

Chapter Five
Believe

Building on Your Clarity of Mind

There can be no doubt but that the mere exercise of clearing your mind makes you far more effective during the day – once cleared, your mind is far more focused on whatever you're doing. In effect, you're just doing what you're doing, rather than thinking about doing it or half-listening to some of the other garbage in your head that normally disrupts your activities. However, you are learning how to clear your mind for an even greater purpose – to reset your mind to bring about the achievement of the goals *you want*, to live the life that you want to live. You set your mind by clearing your mind and then, whilst in that clarity of mind, photographing the pictures of what you want to have or achieve, as if you've got or achieved it already – and leave your subconscious mind to do the rest. That's how it works, that's why clarity of mind is so important, that's how exceptionally successful people operate – that's how you already operate anyway, except you've been operating on other people's programs and pictures and living life based on those current pictures of a life that's "not too bad"!

to succeed... JUST LET GO

Exceptionally Successful People

Much of the research carried out over the last quarter of a century has its roots in the analysis of how athletes scale to the very pinnacle of their chosen sport. And yet, some facts need little research – they're just so obvious! For example, if everybody believes something to be impossible – it will not be achieved; in effect, if we all agree that something's not do-able, no-one can do it. But once even one person believes it to be possible, many start achieving it. One of the best examples of this is the so-called "four-minute mile". Obviously, before Roger Bannister broke this record, nobody had done it! And yet, within a year of his running a sub-four-minute mile, ten other athletes had also achieved it – the mindset, the belief, had altered. What actually happened was that, when other athletes saw one person doing it, they took a photograph of it because it made a big enough impression on their mind, and then they knew it could be done and they could see themselves doing it. The achievement of the athletes that followed Bannister was a mental rather than physical achievement!

But, what of Bannister's achievement in the first place – and what of the world-renowned performances of so many high achievers. It is true to say that, without exception, top performers know, in advance, that they are going to achieve the spectacular. All the top track and field athletes speak of seeing themselves chesting the tape – before the gun goes off. Somehow, top achievers know – they just know! That knowing enables the achievement – that knowing is based on a certainty or belief. And, of course, you and I know that a belief is nothing other than a picture in your subconscious mind – hence their seeing themselves achieving their goal – and a picture is very much a visual thing!

But how did that picture get there in the first place? As we already know, you took most of your pictures when you were a child – that's what normal people do. But most normal people had their spectacular pictures rubbished right at the outset: "When I grow up, I'm gonna play for Manchester United" – "Don't be so stupid, you're gonna be an accountant, just like your father!" or "I'm gonna

Believe

be a movie star when I'm older" – "Don't be so ridiculous, darling, you'll find a nice guy, get married and have children, just like we all did." And so it is that normal people's pictures are not too bad, are of a normal life. Not so the high achievers – and the examples are far too numerous for this book. But let's look at a few and consider the background to spectacular success. But as we do, be careful to understand that your mind works exactly the same as a top achiever's mind – the only difference is the pictures in your album, the programs you're running.

I'm gonna play for Manchester United

A recent TV documentary replayed an interview, for a children's programme, given by a mother and father, twenty-five years ago. In the background, a five- or six-year-old David Beckham, completely rigged out in Old Trafford red, juggled a ball, on his knees, at great peril to the ornaments balanced on the display shelves behind where his parents sat! All that time ago, that young David Beckham was absolutely sure – he simply knew – that, when he grew up, he would play top-flight football, for Manchester United. What's really important about this interview, however, is that his parents whole-heartedly supported their son's dream – they were sure too. No doubt was raised in that young child's mind, no scorn was poured on his dream – his parents, no doubt, were viewed as mildly eccentric by their peers who knew better – young David would end up working on the buses, or the tube, or in Billingsgate fish market, just like all other normal people. Oh, how normal people kill their children before they even have a chance to live.

I'm gonna be a famous singer

Straying not too far from the Beckham story, let's pick up on another documentary recounting the rise to "fame" of the Spice Girls – five ordinary girls who all shared one thing, the certainty that

to succeed... JUST LET GO

their dream would come true. This is not a commentary on their particular brand of music, their clothes, or anything else! This is a serious attempt to enable you, my reader, to understand that if your dream is captivating enough, and is nourished in the right way, even now, it will happen – the only person who can stop it happening is you.

In the course of the documentary, Geri Halliwell, better known in those days as "Ginger Spice", took a picture down from her wall, opened the back of the frame and removed a carefully folded piece of paper. On that piece of paper, as a six- or seven-year-old girl, she had written that she was going to be a famous pop star. So what? I hear you say! Yet, there is a veritable mass of worldwide research into the extent to which you get what you've written down.

I am the greatest

The very best-known example of this is Muhammad Ali – voted the sports person of the Millennium. Much of modern scientific research was inspired by the manner in which this man used his mental capabilities. When he and his management agreed to fight a bout, he would write in his "magic book" what he saw, felt, heard, tasted and smelled in the moment after he had won that fight. In this way, his mind took a photograph of his chosen outcome – and, as he subsequently fought that fight, simply re-ran that program to bring about his chosen outcome, which his subconscious mind already believed had taken place. Bear in mind (if you pardon the pun) that this is how your mind works anyway. But as we've already understood, you run other people's programs and, whilst doing so, think you're in charge of your own life! Chapter 11 deals, in a lot more detail, with writing down what you want to achieve – in language your subconscious mind understands.

Whilst on the subject of Muhammad Ali, it's also interesting to note that, in his own mind, he had a big enough reason to become a top boxer! Someone had stolen his bike, which he had left outside a shop next door to a boxing club. His immediate reaction? He went

Believe

in to the boxing club to learn how to get it back! This seemingly insignificant anecdote is also extremely important, as we'll see in Chapter 11 – you need to have what is for you a compelling reason to achieve your goals.

And finally, Muhammad Ali said "I am the greatest" – not "I'm thinking about becoming the greatest" or "I will be the greatest when I win my next five fights" or "I want to be the greatest" or "I'd love to be the greatest". No – he used the language of the subconscious mind – the present tense – which, as we'll see later, is the only tense your subconscious understands.

I saw myself chesting the tape

Someone else who needs little introduction has, on each of his momentous wins, quite literally seen himself chesting the tape ahead of all his rivals, before each race even started. The multi-gold-medalled Carl Lewis speaks of having a picture in his mind, with all the sensations that go with it – the exhilaration, the wind rushing past, the cacophony of flash bulbs, the roar of the crowd – all before the race starts. Again, the mechanics of what's happening are very simple and defy normal logic – he believes, in his heart and soul, because his subconscious mind has seen the picture and is running the program, that he has already won. His subconscious mind is simply carrying out instructions – just like a computer program! Could it be that simple? They all speak of it and say it is. Yes, it is that simple, assuming you can get your pictures and programs into your subconscious mind. And that, for normal people, is normally an assumption too far!

A man of destiny

Let's keep going – let's really lather on the evidence! To say that the late, great Sir Winston Churchill was a hard-working swot would amount to fraudulent misrepresentation. Winston did not work hard during his school or college days – preferring to spend the greater

to succeed... JUST LET GO

part of his day relaxing. After his student days little changed – he saw no reason to indulge in any of the distractions of normal people, because he simply knew that he had no need for any such nonsense – he knew himself to be a "man of destiny". In his earlier years, he had no idea what that meant – but he knew that, when needed, he would be ready! How right his gut instinct was.

Single-mindedness

All the greats, throughout all the ages, have one thing in common – as the heading suggests. Many of the greats have been single-minded to the detriment of other aspects of their lives or the lives of those around them. I am not holding up what the world regards as "the greats" as your role models – because many simply are not. But, all the research available proves that you must be single-minded to achieve anything worthwhile. What I would add is that it should be your goal to be single-minded at the business of living life to the full, in all its aspects, from moment to moment – or, to re-emphasise what I said about your subconscious mind earlier, in the present tense.

A divided mind always fails. And your mind – as any normal person's mind – is divided almost all of the time, being distracted by useless thought, watching the old "B-movies" of someone else's old programs, never focusing on what you want to achieve, to the exclusion of those distractions, worries and thoughts. That's why normal people's dreams are just dreams – that's why normal people normally are born, live and die within their set of norms.

And, that's why your clarity of mind is everything – not just another form of exercise, not just something that gives you a nice feeling of being relaxed – clarity of mind is the only key to your success, to your successful living. Every successful person has total clarity of mind, single-mindedness, in relation to their goal or goals – you must be the same. This same clarity of mind is the key to changing your beliefs – not all of them, but the ones that are hurting you – to the beliefs that will create the successful life that you want, rather than the life that someone else might have wanted, often with the best will in the world, for you.

Believe

Your Beliefs

What are your beliefs? Your beliefs are simply the things that you have stored in your subconscious mind as undeniable and unshakable truths. You store these truths as pictures, these pictures run your programs – like a detailed stage and script for each zone of your virtual reality computer game.

Yet, you can achieve anything, as long as you believe it. If you can slot your pictures into your subconscious mind as if you have *already achieved them now,* then your subconscious mind simply brings them about. That's how it works. There are simply too many documented cases of people believing that they can achieve something that is unrealistic by so-called normal standards. For example, a doctor in the US operated a postal healing service for more than twenty years. Over that period, in excess of fifteen million people requested various cures. These were not inconsequential requests – they weren't, "I've got an ingrown toe-nail" or, "My hair is curly and I'd like it straight". These were serious requests. "I've got terminal cancer." "I've developed breast cancer." "I've got an inoperable brain tumour." "I have chronic heart disease and hardening of the arteries." In well-documented evidence, in excess of 90 per cent of the people who wrote were cured, within days or weeks of writing to him. He was getting so much mail, that often he would open the "thank-you" letter before the original request. Did he cure them? Or, did they cure themselves? Did their belief cure them? Perhaps, as with Muhammad Ali, the mere effort of writing changed their subconscious mind – re-set it to achieve what they so badly wanted.

Everything that you achieve or fail to achieve in *your life* is purely down to whether you actually believe in what is or is not achievable. Indeed, everything that happens to you and for you in your life is purely down to your belief. One of my wife's tennis companions used to comment, daily, that her breasts were different sizes. She examined her breasts daily, becoming obsessed with the idea that she might develop breast cancer, despite all the tests to the contrary. But years of focus on this possible outcome eventually brought the expected outcome about – you get what you expect, what happens

to succeed... JUST LET GO

to you is what you believe is going to happen you – and, whether you know it or not, that's how belief works, just the same as the spectacularly successful people we spoke of earlier.

Changing Your Beliefs

If you believe that Jesus or Muhammad is God, how do you change that belief? If you believe you're stupid or ugly, how do you change that belief? If you believe that people like you live out their "not too bad" lives getting promoted, buying a bigger house (with a bigger mortgage), getting a pension and dying, how do you change that belief? If you believe that your child couldn't possibly be a world-class sports-person but needs to get a good education and a steady job like everyone else (even though your child might, at least before you knock the belief out of him, believe otherwise), how do you change that belief? If you believe you've got to work really hard to get anything worthwhile, how do you change that belief?

I've touched on a lot of issues there, which we need to just stop and consider before we go any further.

First of all, we all need to be careful to give our children all the encouragement we can – society conspires to grind them down, the least we can do as parents is try to stop the vicious circle of cloning, whereby my parents' programming made me who I think I am and my programming, in turn, will mould my children into normal people. You have to stop this.

Secondly, I've touched on the idea that you have to work hard to get anything worthwhile – that's a complete fallacy, one that is dangerous for your mental health, and helpful to a society that really desperately needs you to conform. Yes, Muhammad Ali, Carl Lewis, all of them, put their heart and soul and long hours into their ultimate achievement – but do people like that see it as *hard work* in the way normal people do? You know the expression "labour of love"? Such people, driven by a belief and a captivating goal, don't work hard, they do everything they have to do to achieve their goals. *Normal people*, on the other hand, find it harder to work on Mondays

Believe

than Fridays! Normal people trudge off to work, to jobs they don't like, thinking that "the system" is unfair. It is these bizarre sideshows of thought that make work hard – not the work itself. What belief does a normal person have driving him or her that makes the so-called rat-race easy? How captivating is your goal? Does it make you want to spring out of bed each morning? Do you find work hard? Would you like to work less and spend more time doing things you enjoy? How about enjoying what you work at, because it has captured your imagination (your subconscious mind) and leads, with the certainty of your belief, towards an exceptionally successful goal? Hard work is a figment of normal people's sick minds!

This leads me directly onto the issue of what you believe constitutes success (we've a whole chapter on this – Chapter 11) for the simple reason that it's none of my business as to what your success should look and feel like – that's solely up to you; you're going to have to take responsibility for that one. This leads me on to one of the key questions.

What Beliefs Do You Change?

Again, I cannot be prescriptive – but, the central answer to this question is obvious. You change the beliefs that are holding you back. And, if you have children, you discard every shred of the beliefs that say that they must exist in the world as defined by your limiting beliefs – otherwise, they'll believe that too (and they might never have the benefit of reading this book in later life!). And, of course, why would you change these beliefs? Because you can achieve unlimited success, according to the beliefs you want, to live the life that you want – otherwise, you'll simply continue living the half-life of a robot dancing to someone else's tune, and, in the process, die an unfulfilled (and possibly bitter) old man or woman.

to succeed... JUST LET GO

How Do You Change Your Beliefs?

You cannot change a single belief by using logical thought in your conscious mind. You cannot change a single belief without being able to deeply access your subconscious mind. You must be able, at will, to access that clarity of mind in which your subconscious mind takes its pictures. Clarity of mind is everything.

Once in that clear state of mind, you then *construct the pictures you want*, to live the life you want, to achieve the success and lifestyle you want. You do this by using your senses (Chapter 6) and using the language of the subconscious mind – covered in many of the chapters to come and already alluded to! From my years of experience in working with my clients, I do not believe in dwelling on the limiting pictures you already have, focusing on them enhances the negative power they hold over you. Your ability to clear your mind, which you must cultivate daily through the exercises in this book, and your consequent ability to take your new pictures are more than enough to bring about the life you want.

Having a goal that captivates your imagination makes the outcome almost inevitable (I deal with useless thoughts in Chapter 7). For example, many people have asked me how I discarded normal living in favour of an idyllic lifestyle of financial freedom high in the French Alps, and say how brave we were to take such a risk, how bold the decisions must have been and how scary it must have been to actually do it (particularly with three young children who spoke no French!). My answer is always the same. I can't remember making any momentous decisions that actually made it happen, it just happened, almost in a daze; I don't remember exactly how it happened. What I do know is that once I knew that it was going to happen, it just happened. Once you know in your heart and soul that something will happen, brick walls won't hold you back, big strong piers won't hold back the tide of progress; what you know will happen becomes inevitable. And, at the risk of being repetitive, that's how your mind operates anyway – but now it's time to do it your way!

Believe

Is It This Simple?

Yes, it is that simple. It's almost too simple: believe you have it and it will be given to you. But, the only reason it sounds stupid is that it is completely contrary to every single thing you have ever been told. Because it is so contrary and so simple it takes a little time to actually take that on board – some people never do. Many people think I'm mad, that I'm not normal. And I can assure you I've no desire to ever be normal again. Exceptionally successful people, who by the very definition are not normal people, know how it works, some instinctively, some through learning it – but they've no desire to be normal either. Why should you?

And, I'm sorry, I can't make it any more difficult! There's no point in making it any more difficult – I know it to be true, I live that way. Some (not all) of my clients know it to be true – they live that way. The world is full of examples of people who have set their minds to achieve the spectacular – they live this way. You live this way anyway. It's just that no-one told you you could choose the programs to run – no-one until now!

And all you have to do is learn how to clear your mind – to become an expert at it. The clarity of mind we've considered in such detail is the cornerstone – the key which unlocks your unlimited potential – enables you to be single-minded in the pursuit of living the perfect life. And that is why the exercises in Chapter 4 – and those that follow in Chapter 6 – are all important.

Chapter Summary

- You learn – and practice – clarity of mind for the purpose of changing your mind and setting it to achieve the life you want.

- This clarity of mind is the only way to access your subconscious to change your current beliefs that limit your ability to achieve.

to succeed... JUST LET GO

- This clarity of mind will enable you to be single-minded, like the many examples of successful people provided in this chapter.

- Your beliefs are merely stored pictures – your clarity of mind enables you take new pictures, the ones you want.

- Ignore your limiting beliefs – don't even consider what they might be – focus only on building your clarity of mind and on the pictures you want to captivate your imagination.

- Achieving what you really, really want is as simple as setting your mind (taking the picture) to believe you already have achieved it.

- No-one has ever told you that it could be this simple – it may take a little getting used to!

Chapter Six
Coming to Your Senses

God gave us at least five senses – and we don't use them. It's really easy to check this out. The next time you're sitting in rush-hour traffic, look around you at the other drivers, their blank stares, their glazed-over expressionless faces, not fully seeing, hearing or experiencing what's going on around them. Next time you're in a busy downtown street or shopping mall, look around you at the people walking past. Mostly, they're looking down – and, it's difficult to take in the wonder of everything you see around you, if you're not looking! Some of them look as if they have the weight of the world on their shoulders, some even mutter to themselves – many are buried in their own little world of the Walkman! Mostly, they're not all there! – they're all over the place. After my workshops, many clients have said to me, "I woke up this morning and heard the birds singing!" But the birds sing every morning – you're just too brain-dead, buried in the useless thoughts of the day ahead. And how many people come back from their holidays (dreading going back to work!) having experienced the beauty of the countryside, because they were relatively relaxed, whereas the beauty of nature is all around them every day.

The horrible truth is that we're senseless – and because we don't use our senses, they've become dulled and we need to resort to giving ourselves "pleasure shots" to feel anything at all. It's time to come to your senses.

to succeed... JUST LET GO

The Language of Your Subconscious Mind

Your subconscious mind uses your five senses to create or represent each of your experiences – hence, psychologists call the senses the five representational systems. In anything you experience, you *see* where you are or what you're doing, you *feel* what it's like to be there, you *hear* what's going on around you, you *smell* the smells and *taste* the tastes at that moment. This is how you took your photographs as a child – and these are the senses you use to take your new photos, the ones you want. This is also how you experience moments of clarity of mind – being out with friends, playing that perfect golf shot, opening your arms to embrace your toddler as she runs towards you, experiencing the intense happiness of "connecting" with nature in a beautiful location, hearing that "dawn chorus" of the birds singing.

And this is how normal people don't experience almost all of the time. The reason is simple – a normal person's mind is somewhere else. Normal people are in too much of a hurry to experience where they are now. Normal people look down whilst walking along and consequently miss most of the beauty around them. Normal people are distracted by self-defeating thoughts and programs, like "the system's unfair", "I hate my job", "my boss doesn't like me", "nobody loves me!", etc., etc. And so a normal person's mind is not there to experience with their five senses. Normal people worry; not only a complete waste of their time and energy, but a mental activity that prevents them from using their five senses in the here and now. But, who wants to be normal?

You (like everyone else) are called upon to be abnormal and to develop and hone your ability to use the language of your subconscious mind, to actively and deliberately use your five senses to focus your clarity of mind. In Chapter 4, you practised exercises that enabled you to clear your mind, clear it of the nonsense and junk to which I've just referred. Now, you have to build on those exercises, bringing your clarity of mind to a new level, enabling you to better experience the reality of where you are now and sharpening your senses to facilitate you taking the photos that you want, to achieve your ideal life.

Coming to Your Senses

Different People – Different Senses

Let's recap on the five representational systems – see, feel, hear, smell and taste. I've put them in that order deliberately, because, as your subconscious mind works from photographs, seeing forms the basis of your experiences, past, present and in the present yet to come – you know the old saying "seeing is believing".

Yet, different people are more or less disposed to the different representational systems. So, for example, to some, the smell of roast beef immediately evokes memories of a childhood Sunday morning, as the Sunday roast filled their nostrils, whilst the smell of seaweed brings another back to their childhood seaside holidays. Hearing an old song on the radio works the magic for someone else who's immediately transported to a first love or a first night drunk! For another, the taste of whiskey might have exactly the same result! The smell of freshly cut grass might be "the sweet smell of success" – an example often quoted by the Scottish racing driver, Jackie Stewart, whose abiding memory of winning one of his Grand Prix was just that smell. The sound of waves crashing on the beach will be far more alluring to one than the sensation of feeling hot sand between another's toes. The sight of a bird in flight may be far more evocative to one person, bringing them back to their childhood on a windy mountain, whilst the taste of lemonade may have exactly the same effect on someone else. In short, we're all a little different. Nonetheless, unless one or more of your senses is absent – in which case your other senses will be heightened anyway – you need to constantly bring all of your senses consciously into play, as a matter of daily exercise. This is a further – and one of the most important and effective – step towards heightening your ability to clear your mind and then keeping your mind clear.

A Gentle Reminder

In case you've forgotten, it's worth remembering why you want to operate with a clear mind. Firstly, and rather logically, the better

to succeed... JUST LET GO

your mind is focused on where you are now and on what you're doing now, the better you'll be able to do it. Although that's stating the obvious, not many people are actually doing what they're doing! Secondly, clarity of mind is the sole key to your subconscious – and you really need that key if you're going to unlock your true and unlimited potential. Bear in mind that this clarity of mind is the state of mind in which you photographed what became your beliefs – and in which you will photograph your chosen beliefs. Thirdly, by focusing on the here and now, with a cleared mind, you begin to tap into your higher energy levels that enhance your ability to spot and take your opportunities and the synchronicity that we'll explore in Chapter 9.

So, read on! Here are three further exercises for you to practise – this time out and about, preferably with your eyes open! The following exercises are designed to bring you to your senses – to enable you become fully involved in the reality of your surroundings now, without the normal distractions, thoughts, worries, phobias, you name it, that normally prevent you from experiencing reality! Because, believe you me, reality exists outside your personal PlayStation game – and it's wonderful.

Clarity of Mind Exercise 1 – Walking

This exercise can be practised anywhere, anytime. All you need is somewhere outdoors where you can take a five- ten- or fifteen-minute stroll. Most people don't go out for a walk simply for the sake of going out for a walk; there's almost always an ulterior motive – "I'm rushing to the bank at lunchtime", "I'm going for a 'power-walk' to lose weight", "I'm on my way to a meeting", "I'm rushing to catch a train". You're going to go for a walk for no reason – other than going for a walk. But, remember, your mind is bombarded by thousands of useless thoughts daily – and many people go for a walk "to think." You're going for a walk to gather your thoughts and discard them! Each time you're distracted by any thought during this exercise, simply start over at step 1!

Coming to Your Senses

1. Clearly *look* at where you are – look at the minute detail of everything you see. Notice the detail on leaves, the shape of clouds, the colour of passing cars, the way light and shade is created by the trees and buildings, the detail of a bird in flight. Focus on seeing everything clearly – as if you were seeing everything for the first time. Take nothing for granted.

2. Consciously feel all the bodily sensations of where you are – how your feet feel in your shoes, the way the breeze feels on your face, the heat of the sun on your head and body, the effort in your muscles as you climb uphill, the inhalation and exhalation of your breath, the feel of a leaf or wall as you stroke your hand over it as you pass by – feel these feelings as if you were feeling them for the first time.

3. Notice the detail in everything you hear – the noise of passing traffic, the hum of car tyres on the road surface, the conversations of passers-by, the singing of the birds, the flow of water as you pass over a river bridge, the rustle of leaves in the breeze, the sound of the waves on the beach and the way they roll the stones, the sound of your feet on the gravel – hear with a clarity you've never noticed before.

4. Deliberately take in all the smells around you – the smell of rotting leaves in autumn, the exhaust from passing traffic, the smell of freshly cut grass, the warming aroma of freshly cooked bread as you pass the bakery, stop and smell the flowers on the next bush you pass – smell each smell as if it were a brand new experience for you.

5. And taste each taste – the salt of a winter walk by the sea, the dryness on your lips as your thirst heightens, the piece of chocolate you've got in your mouth. Notice the detail of each taste – as if each were a completely new taste.

6. Explore everything you pass with the freshness of a child discovering new things at each turn – take nothing for granted.

to succeed... JUST LET GO

7. When (not if) you're distracted by thoughts or if you find yourself dwelling on something or someone you just walked past, go back to step 1!

Clarity of mind exercise 1 – summary

Walk for the sake of walking – you're going nowhere other than on a voyage of discovering where you are now – look, feel, hear, smell and taste and, when distracted, look, feel, hear, smell and taste!

Clarity of Mind Exercise 2 – Driving

Most of us, whilst driving, play the radio, listen to music, talk on our mobile or get increasingly frustrated by the traffic congestion; rush-hour driving can be so stressful as to render a grown man (or woman) useless for hours afterwards. And, of course, if you're stuck in traffic, getting stressed will not stop you being late and will certainly not miraculously clear a path through all the other stressed motorists just for you! Here's how to *benefit* from the perils of rush-hour traffic.

1. Run your hands around the steering wheel, feeling the texture of the wheel's surface on your hands.

2. Look carefully at the colours of the other cars around you – notice the different models, the visual characteristics of different cars.

3. Hear the rise and fall of the engine noise as you accelerate and decelerate and change gears.

4. Smell the fresh smell of your new car, the stale smell of a smoker's car, the oily smell of your old banger – delete as appropriate!!! And carefully notice the taste in your mouth.

Coming to Your Senses

5. Feel the connection, through your foot on the accelerator, to the engine.

6. Hear the noise of the other traffic around you – particularly the swish of other vehicles passing you in the opposite direction.

7. See the expression on the faces of other drivers stuck in stationary traffic.

8. Look at the trees, their leaves, the buildings, the colour of the traffic lights – take in your surroundings, as you pass by.

9. You'll notice that you'll begin to notice other things that you haven't noticed before – like birds singing, the clarity with which you can hear pedestrians talking, the smile from another driver whose eye you caught.

10. Whenever you get distracted by useless thought, start over with step 1!

Note that this is not a recipe for distracting you from the business of driving – quite the opposite, most motorists are so distracted by thoughts, worries of being late, reminders of things they should do later or forgot to do earlier, the stress of heavy traffic, all the way to "road-rage", this exercise will actually heighten your senses of where you are in the here and now – which is the most important place to be when you're driving.

Clarity of mind exercise 2 – summary

Avoid stress and heighten your mental awareness – clarity of mind – whilst driving by focusing on, in particular seeing, feeling and hearing where you are now.

to succeed... JUST LET GO

Clarity of Mind Exercise 3 – Eating and Drinking

Nowadays, too many of our meals are taken on-the-run – many don't have breakfast at all, lunch is often a snatched sandwich, or worse, one stuffed into your mouth whilst walking back to the office – and "TV dinners" and ready-to-cook meals are ingested whilst watching TV. Yet, eating and drinking affords us – as all the mystics would have it – one of our greatest opportunities to not just use but indulge our senses.

1. Deliberately reserve an ample amount of time for nothing other than eating each meal of the day – preferably with someone whose company you enjoy. However, if you're on your own, all the following steps are equally applicable.

2. Before you start, take time to see each of the items before you – noticing the different colour and texture of the various components that make up your meal. All the great chefs tell us that presentation is everything and that the enjoyment of good food is as much a function of what we see as what we eat.

3. With each mouthful of food that you take, deliberately chew slowly, noticing the textures and the different flavours and how these flavours react with the different areas of the surface of your tongue. Savour each mouthful slowly.

4. Stop to consciously consider the smell of what you're eating and how that smell interacts with your seeing and tasting.

5. Let each mouthful of drink roll around on your tongue, feeling the sparkle of the liquid dance on your taste buds – this works just as well with tap water as it does with a fine wine!

6. Even your hearing comes into play – particularly if you're eating a sizzling Chinese dish! But, that aside, pay attention to the clinking of the glass, tableware and cutlery as you go about the business of enjoying your meal.

Coming to Your Senses

7.   And, if you're sharing your meal with someone else, then there's their good company, their appearance, the sound of their voice and their appreciation of the food to enjoy as well.

8.   Always take some time to relax – even if it's only five minutes – and do nothing, after you've finished, other than savouring the delight of time well spent – in the here and now, using all the senses God gave you.

Clarity of mind exercise 2 – summary

Avoid indigestion, stress and that ulcer – take your time and deliberately enjoy each meal, seeing, tasting, smelling, feeling and hearing your way through a good meal.

Reaction to the Exercises

There are some pretty obvious reactions to these exercises, which are reason enough in themselves for practising them. You feel less stressed, less rushed, more relaxed and more appreciative. All of my clients comment that they have never gone for a walk, simply for the sake of being there, walking. They report what they, at first, describe as unusual (maybe, abnormal!) results – they see things they've never seen before (but that were always there!), they report greater clarity of hearing and an intensified sense of smell – and a greater feeling of connectedness to where they are and well-being. They also notice that others notice them! Some have reported that passers-by either smile involuntarily or actually say hello – in one case, a passer-by thanked one of my clients! For what, you might ask. I would suggest, for actually being there. Have you ever noticed that there are some people who walk into a room and immediately give everyone else a lift, immediately raise the energy in that room? Using normal language, we would describe such a person as having

to succeed... JUST LET GO

presence or charisma. That's because they're really there – they're all there – and we all notice it. It's so abnormal to come across someone who's all there, no wonder someone said thank you!

Progressing

Between the exercises in Chapter 4 and here, you should be able to get to the point where you can, quite literally, switch yourself on! Clearing your mind, freeing it from normal useless thoughts is not an act of tuning out – it's all about you tuning in – to the wonder of reality in this moment. And your becoming an expert, an exponent, of clarity of mind must be your goal. You can then build further on your deeper clarity of mind by communicating with your subconscious, in its language, to take the pictures – and subsequently run the programs – that you want, your pictures and your programs of *your* ideal life.

Visualising the Outcome

You communicate with your subconscious, firstly, by creating a clear and colourful view of your goal – you provide your subconscious with a Technicolor picture that will impress it. Your subconscious mind is, not surprisingly, like a child's mind, the more exciting, colourful and impressive your picture, the greater the impression it will make on your subconscious. It's just like when you were young and impressionable – as we've already learned, you originally took your pictures of what made an impression on you as a child, because you experienced, as a child, clarity of mind all of the time.

So, once you have developed your ability to spend periods of time – maybe only five minutes – in a clear state of mind, you're ready to begin the work of impressing your pictures on your mind, of setting your mind to run your programs, to achieve your chosen goals.

You visualise your chosen outcome by using your five senses as you've already learned through practising the exercises in this

Coming to Your Senses

chapter – don't worry (which is a useless pastime anyway!), you'll be provided with step-by-step instructions in Chapter 11.

Say, for example, like one of my clients, you had a goal of wanting to live in a particular type of house, with large grounds, old trees, a gravel driveway. You would simply see yourself – through your own eyes – maybe, driving into your driveway, seeing the sun on the attractive stone façade, hearing the gravel crunch under your car's tyres, feeling your feet on the gravel as you step out of the car, seeing the light dance in the sun and shade created by the old trees overhead, seeing the detail on the old front door as you walk up the drive, etc., etc. – you get the picture?

Now

But you don't create your picture on the basis that you want to live, or (worse) you'd love to live in a house like that, or someday you will live in that house. You might as well speak Martian to your subconscious mind – it just doesn't understand. Your picture has to be created based on the fact – or belief – that you live in that house already, that you live there now. Now, your subconscious mind understands!

Your Subconscious Mind Does the Rest

Not only does your subconscious understand, but left alone without the interference of useless thoughts like "What do I have to do next?", "Why has nothing happened yet?", "When will something happen?", "I bet you nothing will happen!" your subconscious will bring your picture into reality. Don't be surprised at this – it's how your mind works anyway, we've already discussed that! It's like that perfect golf shot. If you just stop thinking about it and just let it happen, your subconscious mind just goes and does it! It's how you are living your life today anyway. What is happening to you today, what happened to you yesterday, is the result of you having

to succeed... JUST LET GO

known in advance that what was going to happen happened! All this happened subconsciously, you've no idea that that's what happened, but that is what happened and what happens every day – you get what you expect.

Your job is to set your mind to the things that you want, as if you already have them and let your mind do the rest. More to the point, set your mind to the higher things that you want and everything else looks after itself. (We'll discuss those higher things in Chapter 11.)

Evidence of your subconscious mind's abilities abounds. For example, a research experiment was undertaken to prove that the mind alone can control pain. Four volunteers underwent serious surgery without anaesthetic. It proved the mind's ability to control pain, or actually to obliterate pain altogether. This research also proved that the volunteers experienced no pain, not only during the operation, but at any stage during the recovery period and that they recovered twice as quickly as someone who had been operated on under anaesthetic. It really is a case of mind over matter.

Write It Down

There are also volumes upon volumes of validated research that testify to the apparently unbelievable power of writing down what you want. I've already mentioned Muhammad Ali and Geri Halliwell – but in my own work I've many, many examples of my own.

During a springtime workshop, Suzanne wrote down the following: "I'm sitting in my new house and I'm looking at the polished wooden floor and I can see the reflection of the lights from the Christmas tree on the floor, I can smell the cup of coffee in my hand and I can taste the coffee. I look out through the window and in the gravel driveway I see my metallic green BMW. I'm sitting here so happily with my boyfriend, and his parents and my parents are all going to spend New Year's Eve with us, all together." She went on to write, in greater detail, as to the colour of the furniture, the decoration, how relaxed she felt, etc., etc. She mentioned to me afterwards that all the parents coming together would be a big deal, because they

Coming to Your Senses

didn't approve of the relationship. In return, I pointed out to her that, in her job, she was more likely to be the first Irishwoman on the moon than drive a BMW – never mind a green one! In addition, Suzanne and her boyfriend had bought a site to build a house – but had run out of money, with the obvious consequences!

Nine months later, I was sitting in my office on the Monday of Christmas week, and I answered the phone to Suzanne. She said to me: "I was sitting at home yesterday morning, having a cup of coffee with my boyfriend, looking at the wooden floor, looking at the Christmas lights on the floor. I looked out the window at my green BMW, and said, 'Oh my God, this is exactly what I wrote down'. I spent the rest of the day looking the for page I'd written, because I couldn't believe it. And I kept saying to myself, 'I'll have to ring Willie', to the point where my boyfriend said, 'Who the f***'s Willie?'"

She had, in May, been with one of her customers who made her a job offer she couldn't refuse, completely out of the blue, giving her a car allowance to buy her own car. As she drove home that evening, she stopped to get petrol at a garage that had a green BMW in the window, which she bought on the spot. She then told me all four parents were coming over on Christmas Eve (OK, it should have been New Year's Eve!).

Many of my clients have had the same type of experience. For example, another client, John, spoke to me about his dream house. I told him he should write it down, draw a word picture for his mind. After he wrote it down, being a classically educated businessman who understood all the most important things about strategic planning(!), he then asked me "Should I now make a list out of the 'milestones' I have to achieve towards getting this house, so that I can set down an 'Action Plan'?" Wow! In reply I asked him what his first milestone would be, to which he replied that he would need to set about getting a certain amount of money – he then, of course, admitted that if he did this he'd immediately discard his dream as a nonsense – he could never get his hands on that kind of money.

Eight weeks later, on a Saturday morning, John phoned me to ask if I could meet him, so that he could drive me out to see the house

to succeed... JUST LET GO

he'd just seen – one that perfectly fitted his written description. He'd never seen the house previously, didn't know it existed; it was not on the market (an estate agent friend of his asked him if he would like to have a look before they advertised it) and yet, when he drove up the driveway, there it was – word for word. And the price John paid was a good deal less than he might have thought was necessary, because the owner needed to sell quickly!

Free Your Mind – Set Your Mind

The answer is crystal clear – free your mind from the rubbish of "milestones" and "strategic planning" – free your mind from the restrictions of useless thought and worry – free your mind from limits imposed by normal programming. Then, set your mind to achieve the goals it believes you already have and let it do the rest. Whatever you do, don't interfere by indulging in the useless thoughts that plague the normal mind.

Chapter Summary

- You must deliberately use your five senses – they are the representational systems your subconscious uses to take its pictures and run its programs.

- Set time aside to practise your clarity of mind exercises – see, feel, hear, smell and taste each experience, as if it is a new experience, as you do your exercises.

- Take every opportunity you can to practise – you must become an expert who can switch yourself on at will!

- Begin to understand that to re-program yourself – to install your chosen pictures – you visualise or picture yourself in the outcome, seeing, feeling, hearing, smelling and tasting what it's like to be there, now.

Coming to Your Senses

- Begin to understand the importance of writing down your goals – in the language of your subconscious mind, as if you already *have* achieved your goal – now.

Chapter Seven
Stop Thinking

Thought is a tool of your conscious mind. Useless thought destroys normal people's lives, by clouding their view of where they are now and their vision of where they want to be. It colours their view of the world – much like a pair of dark glasses – and provides them with the apparent comfort of procrastination as a substitute for getting on with what they should be doing. In short, useless thought fragments your mind and, as we already know, a divided mind always fails – only those who are single-minded achieve anything worthwhile.

The Nature of Thought

Normal people allow themselves, for most of their lives, to be literally dragged around by the nose by whatever thoughts are rattling around their conscious mind. Tens of thousands of random thoughts wander into your conscious mind every day – it's easy to get distracted! But, make no mistake about it, it is you who allow yourself to be distracted. Each thought, of itself, is powerless; you give each thought its power by thinking about it, by giving it your energy. In giving a thought your energy you get in the way of what you're supposed to be doing at that moment. For example, if you're playing tennis and you're being beaten off the court by your opponent, as you change ends, simply mention, "Your forehand is really brilliant today, how are you doing it?" He'll start thinking about how he's playing his forehand, and once he starts thinking about it – it's gone!

to succeed... JUST LET GO

In short, your subconscious mind is distracted by the thinking going on in your conscious mind; uncontrolled useless thought distracts from doing.

Worse, what if what you're thinking is particularly useless? You distract yourself completely into the twilight zone of discontent, worry and even panic. Remember Dave in Chapter 1 – the man with sixty bosses? The first part of Dave's day in the office was spent thinking about all the things he had to do – he also wasted a lot of energy thinking about how impossible it would be to get all those things done. Dave literally thought himself into a panic each morning. And, of course, Dave's not unique. Normal people go to work thinking about how they dislike their work, or how unfair the system is, or what they'll do at the weekend, distracting themselves completely from doing their work, which makes their work more difficult and more tedious and merely confirms to them how right they were in the first place to dislike it! No wonder stress – the illusionary product of useless thought – is predicted, by none other than the World Health Organisation, to be the major killer of the twenty-first century!

Useful and Useless Thought

Now, let's be careful to distinguish between useful and useless thought. Many of us are actually paid to think – it's part of our job. For example, a business person will think through the pros and cons of a particular strategy, before deciding. This type of thinking may (only may!) be useful. Consider how many successful business decisions throughout the ages have been made on gut instinct – and how many dreadful ones have been carefully thought through! And, whilst we all need to equip ourselves for our chosen work or profession, this constitutes the learning and application of knowledge, rather than the process of thinking. And how often have you solved a problem by thinking about it? More often than not, the solution occurs to you when you're doing something else – when you're not thinking about it.

Stop Thinking

Most of my clients manage other people – with all the related difficulties. When faced with dealing with a personnel problem, a difficult employee or resolving conflict, most give themselves lots of time to think about it – a wonderful euphemism for simply putting off doing what is often inevitable and rarely relished; thinking about it is just an excuse.

And how often do you put off doing something to enable you sleep on it? – "Oh, everything will be clearer in the morning!!" Interestingly enough, when we sleep on something, we don't give it any thought. It is our subconscious mind, whilst we sleep, that brings about the clarity – that's what your subconscious mind is really good at!

One of my clients suggested that a useful thought might be, when standing in the middle of the road faced with an out-of-control articulated truck speeding towards him, "I had better get out of the way!" But, that's a reaction, based on instinct – in this case, the instinct for survival – and not a thought.

All the great philosophers spent their lives thinking about the meaning of life – whereas if you actually live your life with a mind free of useless thought, focused in the present moment, the answer to the eternal question is immediately and abundantly clear. You're here to live your life to the full – in the here and now. All the philosophers' thought came to nought.

When originally drafting this chapter, it was entitled "Effective and Useless Thinking". But, now that I've thought about it, I can't think of a useful thought!! Many experts in the field of self-development and self-motivation encourage positive thinking – and, it must be said, that beats negative or useless thinking any day. But, from the earlier chapters, you and I know that the real action – the mental activity that creates your life – goes on in your subconscious mind, beyond thought. And this is where you should spend your life – in *clarity of mind*, with a subconscious mind free to bring about your ideal life, achieving your greatest ambitions.

to succeed... JUST LET GO

Useless Thought

But that's not how it is – at least for the 96 per cent of the population we call normal. Normal people let their thoughts run riot, giving them free reign to divert them from doing, to confirm how "not too bad" life is and to make all their dreams stay dreams. We humans are expert in the art of useless thinking. Useless thought abounds – from the mundane to the seriously dysfunctional. The mundane – you're sitting at an important meeting, supposedly working, but actually saying to yourself, "I must put the plug on the kettle tonight!" Of course, when you get home, you've completely forgotten (you're probably exhausted from not being at the meeting!) so you do nothing – and two weeks later your wife will say, "Why didn't you put the plug on the kettle?" Random thoughts like these things are pestering you all the time, distracting you from the job in hand. It is up to you whether you let them or not.

Mundane Thoughts – Mundane Lives

Picture it – you're sitting in the kitchen with a mug of tea. It's breakfast time, a couple of days before your holidays – and you're in great form. The mail arrives – and there it is, your monthly bank statement. It's not as if it's news to you – you pretty much already know how your finances are. But, as you look at your balance, you suddenly think of the school fees you'll have to pay after your holidays. Will you be able to afford them? And why has your bonus not been paid yet? You thought it might be in the bank before your holidays and it's not. What if the company is suffering from the market downturn you hear about every day on the news as you're driving into work? What if you don't get your bonus? God, things are tight as they are and you were counting on that bonus. What if the company really is in trouble and not only is there no bonus – what if you lose your job? You really should have thought longer about it before you bought your new house and took on that big new mortgage! It's your wife's (or husband's) fault – you should have listened to nobody but yourself.

Stop Thinking

Nothing changed between the time just before you got your bank statement and the time you read it. Reading it didn't increase or decrease your overdraft; reading it didn't affect the financial fortunes of your employer; reading your statement didn't increase or decrease the amount of school fees you have to pay after your holidays. And yet, suddenly, you're broke – on the breadline! Suddenly the dark storm clouds of financial ruin have obliterated the holiday sunshine that filled your being only five minutes earlier. Nothing changed – except the bizarre chain of events in your head, what you thought, the mental process that normal people swear by!

Re-arranging the Deckchairs on the *Titanic*

Dermot is a salesman – and his daily routine is a struggle. Like every good salesman, Dermot has his list of "prospects" – and every day Dermot shuffles his list of prospects with all the panache of a casino blackjack dealer! He's a man under pressure – that's why he spends the first half hour of every working day filling his head with the nonsense (rubbish that further proves that the world is, at best, not too bad) that fills the pages of the daily newspapers. Dermot then has a cup of coffee with a couple of the lads who aren't as hard-working as he is (the guys who get into work after he's finished reading the paper!) and wastes enormous amounts of energy discussing office politics – who's done what to whom, what if this happens, what if that happens – again confirming to himself and all concerned that the system is unfair and life is not too bad. Notice that, after all this time, Dermot has done none of what he's supposed to be doing. (How many useless thoughts have you spotted so far?) Then, at last, Dermot gets down to business. He looks at the list of people he's planned to telephone today to set up appointments with them. There are a dozen prospects on that list. Like all good salesmen, Dermot spends the next fifteen minutes thinking about who he should phone first. He then re-orders the entire list until it looks like less of a chore to him. (Although he won't admit it to himself, Dermot doesn't like phoning people.

to succeed... JUST LET GO

(Now there's one of the most destructive and common useless thoughts of all – "I don't like my job".) Satisfied that he's got the list in the right order, Dermot makes himself the cup of coffee he'll need whilst talking to his prospects. He's then ready to make his first call – well, almost. He thinks about the person he's about to phone and goes over in his mind what he'll say to him. What if (two of the most useless words in the English language!) his prospect says he has a problem or can't decide at the moment? Well, Dermot spends a few minutes thinking about this as well. At last Dermot does what he's actually paid to do. He calls prospect number one – and gets his voicemail!! He repeats the same process with the next three or four people on the list (none of whom he actually gets to speak to) and retires to the pub for lunch – exhausted!!

Thought stops you doing. How many times in conversation has it occurred to you to say something witty – or important – but, by the time you've thought about it, the conversation has moved on and the opportunity has passed? How many times have you wanted to do something exciting or dashing – but thought the better of it? How often have you wanted to approach someone, make a speech, take the initiative at work or at play – but thought yourself inadequate? And how many New Year's resolutions, goals and dreams lie unfulfilled, because you thought about them and logical thought told you it would be easier and more comfortable to stay just as you are?

Dreams – More Useless Thoughts

I've actually lost count of the people who have said to me "I was thinking about setting up my own business – I have this wonderful idea". But then you start thinking about the risks involved, you think about what you've got to lose and what if it all went wrong. And that's how ordinary people's dreams never become their reality – they won't let them, they're more comfortable thinking their way through what they call their life. Only abnormal people's dreams come true – people who are so certain of what they must do that neither thought, logic nor reason will dissuade them. For normal

Stop Thinking

kids playing football, it's far easier to sit at home watching the Premiership on the television than it is to make the effort to train to be another Wayne Rooney – because they think they couldn't do that. They think that normal people largely live and die where they were born (socially, financially, geographically) – and, of course, they're right, normal people do. Big dreams are just that for normal people – their parents told them that, their schoolteachers told them that, the rubbish they read in the newspapers everyday tells them that; their friends not only tell them that, they live that way too. Normal people see normality all around them and so they think they cannot rise above it. It's like the Chinese saying "We grow old because we see those around us growing old" – you're normal because everyone around you is normal and you can think of a thousand reasons why it's safer to be normal.

Comparative Thought

Sally phoned me one evening and said to me, "Oh God! I don't think I can go to work tomorrow I don't think I can get out of bed tomorrow, my relationship has just broken up." I asked when this had happened in reply she said, "About three o'clock this afternoon."

I replied, "That's in the past, it's very recent past, but it is the past." I was then told that she couldn't face life without her partner – already, she was lonely. If you are operating in clarity of mind, in the here and now, using your five senses, could you be lonely? If, on the other hand, you thought about how it was before this person left you, compared to how it is now, without that person, then you would experience a feeling of loneliness. But this feeling is based in a thought – a comparative thought. And comparative thought is always a waste of time. Don't get me wrong, however, I am not suggesting for one moment that we remove ourselves from our feelings (of loss, in this case) but when we start thinking about it, we wallow in it – all brought about by thought. As a matter of interest, Sally called me the following day and said that, of course, I was right – life goes on. But, for most people, life doesn't go on.

to succeed... JUST LET GO

Normal people waste a lot of time on comparative thinking, even in positive situations. Kevin, who had just made an investment gain way beyond the norm, spends all his energy complaining that he could have made an awful lot more – "What if I'd made that investment when I heard about it first". Instead of rejoicing in his good fortune, he's wallowing in the money he thinks he lost! John, who has just turned in his fourth good year in business, is continually distressed – "I wish I'd set up that business ten years earlier." Stephen, who recently re-married (an event which has made him ten years younger and greatly improved what was previously serious ill-health) continually says to me "Look at the fifteen years I wasted with Mary" – and it's eating away at him. And David, whose "numbers" recently came up in the National Lottery is wasting every ounce of energy he has – "What if I'd bought a ticket!"

Other People's Thoughts

Remember Sally? The other thing she said to me on the phone was "And, what will other people think of me?" This is one of the most perverse forms of useless thought going – thinking about what other people are thinking! Don't worry about what others think about you – they don't think about you, they're thinking of themselves and what you think of them! Is your opinion of yourself and your own worth based on what other people think of you? If even a little bit of it is, then you're in serious trouble. Normal people don't give a damn about you – and as long as you're normal, the same holds true for you. Normal people think "They must be better than us – they have a bigger car", or a bigger house, or better holidays, or she's thinner, her hair's nicer – "I wonder what they think of my hair", my figure, my car, my house, my job. And yet all these things not only have nothing to do with who you really are – and the unlimited potential that you have, just waiting to be tapped – they take up a vast amount (or most) of normal people's thoughts. As a result, the marketing industry and the consumer society have created a world where normal people waste their

Stop Thinking

lives in comparative thought and thinking about the comparative thoughts of other normal people. Is it possible that all normal people are mad because none of this has anything remotely to do with reality. But bear in mind all these bizarre thoughts create your reality – or, at least, you think they do!

Seriously Defective Thinking

So far we've considered the thoughts of what you might call normal people – and they're scary enough! But, for an increasing number of people, the world created by their thoughts presents both them and the wider world with some more fundamental problems. Stress is now costing all major Western economies vast amounts of money in terms of workdays lost and the financial burden on the public health sector. And stress actually doesn't exist other than in the mind of the person who thinks they're suffering from stress. I do not say this lightly – research has proved that not only do our thoughts directly relate to our heart-rate, but that, through conscious thought, we can alter our own heart-rate. Research was undertaken in the US by doctors carrying out post-mortems on those lost in action in the Vietnam war (it was found that eighteen- and nineteen- year- olds had similar levels of cholesterol to patients in the coronary care units in East Coast America), which found that, without exception, patients who had suffered a major heart attack could always give the doctor a reason for it – "I lost my business", "My wife just left me", "I was working eighteen-hour days"; their own view of their lives, or how they thought they were, played the differentiating role between health and illness. And the enormous growth in the extent of substance abuse can only be related to people looking for their latest "kick" or "fix" because they don't think that life can give it to them; they think there's no other way to pleasure when what they should be seeking is happiness rather than pleasure.

Of course, comparative thinking has also given the world Protestant against Catholic, Black against White, Jew against Arab,

to succeed... JUST LET GO

Capitalist against Communist; not one of these would know the other were different if they hadn't been told – if they didn't think they were different.

The Cancer of Thought

Normal people have seriously defective thoughts as well. These thoughts enter your mind so regularly they become like background noise, always there, always hindering your "best efforts" (which will never be good enough if you cannot control your useless thoughts and cut off their energy supply – the energy you give them). These are the kind of background thoughts that give you all those bad habits – the ones that you make your New Year's resolutions about – like shouting at the children because you need the space to think, like sitting at your desk paralysed by the list of things you have to do instead of actually doing them, like thinking "nobody loves me" (yes, normal people actually say something that bizarre), or "nobody cares", "I hate my job", "I hate my marriage", "I hate my life" – a load of garbage born out of useless thought. But garbage that ruins people's lives.

Thought delays or completely stops you doing. Thought stops you realising what it's like to be fully alive now, in reality. Yet, thinking changes nothing in reality – it only changes your own state of mind, invariably for the worse.

State of Mind

Everyone's in a state of mind all of the time. Stop to consider this – sometimes, you're in good form, bad form, nervous, confident, happy, relaxed, on-edge, mentally exhausted, sad, depressed, elated, eager, lethargic, in-love, out-of-love (often with the same person in quick succession!). What controls your state of mind? The answer is obvious – or should be at this stage. You control your state of mind. This starts the moment you wake up in the morning. If, like most normal people, you're dragged from your sleep each morning by

Stop Thinking

an alarm clock, you're already 1–nil down before the day's game even kicks off. The big problem is that you take this for granted, as if you're not in control of your own mind and that there's nothing you can do to set your mind appropriately for the day ahead. You should set your mind each morning, in the same way as you wash, brush your teeth and dress each morning – but no-one ever told you that. Most people are shocked awake each morning into a state of mind bordering on stress (some bordering on panic) before their day really gets going at all. Consider your normal "bad day". A couple of things start to go wrong: you get stuck in traffic, the coffee machine isn't working when you get to the office, you waste half-an-hour looking for a document and when you find it, you pull it from its file and the whole file falls all over the floor. Stupid little things get on your nerves so, by five o'clock, you've had a bad day. There was nothing you could do about it – it was "just one of those days". Wrong. If you're stressed by the traffic, who put you in that mood – you did, your state of mind isn't the traffic's fault! If you're grumpier on a Monday morning than a Friday, whose fault is that – it's yours, the day of the week had nothing to do with it! If you're more confident chatting up that guy or girl after you've had a couple of drinks – who made you less confident in the first place? Do you see a pattern emerging?

How normal people feel is determined by their automatic reactions and their thoughts – technically, normal people are mad, they're not in control of their own minds. For example, you arrive at a social gathering in a new suit; you feel good about yourself if a friend says, "Wow, where'd you get that suit?" But if they'd said, "Oh, where'd you get that suit?", or looked at you and said nothing at all, you feel self-conscious. Your state of mind fluctuates with the reaction of others – who are only thinking about themselves! Yet, this is how you live your life – if someone compliments you, you feel good, if someone ignores you, you feel bad, if someone says they like your new car, you feel good. And, yet, it is you who decide on your state of mind. If you let other people dictate your state of mind, that's a decision on your part too – a decision to abdicate your responsibility for yourself.

to succeed... JUST LET GO

Cast your mind back to Dave (of sixty bosses!) again. I have another client, Steve, who has an almost identical job to Dave. Steve gets up even earlier than Dave and is at his desk by seven o'clock each morning. Why? Because Steve likes to finish around three o'clock in the afternoon! He, too, has about sixty people reporting to him. On average, Steve is abroad every second weekend. I ring him up and say to him: "Where were you last weekend?" "I was at the Belgian Grand Prix" or "I was with some friends in Copenhagen" or "I'm just going out the door, to Argentina!" The difference between Dave and Steve is purely their perspective – their state of mind.

Remember super-salesman Dermot? He actually met clients whilst in a negative state of mind – "I don't really like this guy, but I have to do business with him." Imagine how impressed Dermot's client is. Having a positive state of mind is so important in selling; if I go in to your office, my state of mind will be subconsciously apparent to you. If I'm negative, by the time I leave your office, how will you feel? If your state of mind fluctuates with outside people or events – so do all other normal people's states of mind. State of mind is contagious. A shared state of mind drags world economies into recession – how often have you read that the stock markets and currency rates are driven by confidence or sentiment? A shared state of mind enabled Hitler to "achieve" what he did and a shared state of mind has enabled "second-division" teams the world over to conquer giants!

Now, you know better than normal people – you know that, already, even as you read this, you're in a state of mind. You know that you can – and must – choose your state of mind any time and be aware of your state of mind all of the time.

Single-mindedness

How can you be single-minded with all this useless thought going on in your head? The thinking that we do stops us doing, the thoughts to which we give our energy, that create our state of mind, create a life for us that is a faint shadow of reality. Our minds are so all-over-

Stop Thinking

the-place that we cannot be single-minded, like abnormal, successful people are. Your thoughts conspire along with your programs to create your life. And yet, each time you use your energy for a useless thought, that is a decisive act on your part – you may do it subconsciously, but then, who's in charge? You choose your own thoughts – you choose your own life. And until you decide that you're in charge, you'll be like all normal people, living a life that's not too bad, when your own unlimited potential lies one thought below the surface – and your ideal life only one step away.

Choose Your Life

How do you choose your thoughts? How do you banish useless thoughts? What should be your state of mind – and how do you achieve it? You already know the answers to these questions! Armed with the knowledge you now have, you'll recognise a useless thought at twenty paces! And when you recognise a useless thought for what it is, you discard it. You discard it by choosing not to think – in other words, you don't select a counter-thought, that only muddles the mind further. You choose not to think by focusing on where you are, and what you're supposed to be doing in the here and now, using your five senses.

Let your state of mind be clarity of mind. This beats a positive state of mind any day, because a positive state of mind is born out of positive thoughts – and your unlimited potential is beyond thought, beyond reason, beyond logic. That's why the exercises in chapters 4 and 6 are all important. They free your mind from useless thought, from artificially created states of mind and from your programs to see reality for what it really is, to experience being in the here and now to the full and to give your subconscious mind free rein to do all your doing and bring about the life you want – free from worry, free from the nonsense that normal people take as reality.

to succeed... JUST LET GO

Chapter Summary

- Thinking about doing something delays or stops you from doing it.

- Useless thoughts fragment your mind, creating a not-too-bad world of stress, doubt, worry and under-achievement.

- Your thoughts create your state of mind, which determines how you feel about yourself and your world. You let your state of mind vary with external factors that have nothing to do with reality.

- Seriously useless thoughts create seriously deficient lives – and our state of mind's contagion can create world upheaval.

- The single-mindedness required for successful living is beyond the grasp of the mind cluttered by useless thoughts and the self-sabotaging states of mind they create.

- You must free your mind from all this – by choosing not to think useless thoughts and by choosing clarity of mind as your state of mind.

- You must use your senses to ground you in the here and now.

PART THREE

Welcome to the Real World

Chapter Eight
The Importance of Now

One Thursday I played tennis against John – a weekly, closely fought battle! However, on this particular afternoon, I won 6–2, 6–0 in fifty minutes, without breaking sweat. As we came off the court, John said, "I'm sorry, I had an argument with my secretary before I came up here – I spent most of the match going over it in my head." So, there he was, out on the tennis court, supposed to be enjoying himself – when his mind was not only somewhere else but actually torturing him by re-playing something unsavoury that had happened in the past. John's body was on the tennis court and his mind was somewhere else. And John is by no means unique – in fact, John is normal. Most of my clients who are golfers admit, though not freely, to spending the greater part of their time on the golf course feeling guilty! Guilty that they should be in the office doing all the things they think of while they're supposed to be golfing. Guilty that their golf takes up too much time on a Saturday, when they should be carrying out their fatherly duties. Their body is on the golf course but their mind is, actually, all over the place. We've plenty of expressions in the English language to describe this phenomenon: "He's all over the place." "I'm at sixes and sevens!" "He's not all there!" "My mind wandered."

How many times does your mind wander on a normal morning – before you even get to the office? And, whose fault is it? (By the way, you know the answer to this!) Where can you be at the moment? The answer is abundantly simple and rarely obvious – you can only be here, right now.

to succeed... JUST LET GO

And, yet our lives are lived – if that's the right word – in a twilight zone, in the shadowlands of absentmindedness where our head is absent without leave! If you cannot be anywhere else other than here, what's the point of distracting yourself, of deliberately (because this is a decision you make from moment to moment, albeit subconsciously) preventing yourself being the very best you can be, doing the very best you can do, here, now?

Not Doing What You're Doing?

The biggest disadvantage you have in life, why you don't succeed beyond the pathetic little norms that normal thought aspires to, is you're not doing what you're doing. You're not in the here and now. And, yet, every great mind, every great mystic, states (the obvious) that reality, in all its wonder, is in the here and now.

First of all, let's consider this from the position of ordinary logic. You are far more effective and efficient if you focus on what you're doing, to the exclusion of all useless thought and distraction, whilst you're doing it. That makes logical sense. If you have a report to write, it will be completed quicker if you actually write it (rather than putting it off on the pretence that you need to think about writing it!). If you've a phone call to make, it will be done much quicker if you do it, rather than think about it or think about doing other things (and not do them either) first. If you've a game of golf or tennis or football to play, you'll play much better if you actually focus on being there, playing, rather than letting your mind wander. If your children are so looking forward to you coming home from work, you're far better being there, playing with them than pretending to play with them whilst you re-run the trials and tribulations of a day-at-the-office or, worse, screaming at them and telling them that you're tired, you can't play with them this evening. All these things should go without saying; they're so obvious – and so rarely happen! You shouldn't go into a room and look at a colleague (or loved one!) and say to yourself "I don't like this guy" or "She's annoyed me, I don't care about her". If you do, you're not all there – you're

The Importance of Now

looking at the situation through a thought that does not relate to the present moment; you're wasting your energy on an un-reality being played out in your own head. It is incredible the amount of energy that is wasted in disliking other people, disliking the "system", worrying about "What if?" – so that you spend your time in meetings and discussions not being there but looking through your thoughts, like looking at a beautiful day through dark glasses (and then claiming that everything's dull!).

If people in large organisations actually spent their energy on doing what they were paid to do, next year's targets would not be a logical extension of this year's targets, they might be a hundred times this year's target. Because if you actually were to do what you were supposed to do, how much better would you be at it?

For example, I was working with Paul who was preparing for an interview. He told me that he felt he'd made no impression at previous interviews he'd done – "I was at an interview a couple of weeks ago and I was there for an hour and a half and, you know, I failed to make any impression at all." When I asked him what happened during the interview, he replied – "I don't remember an awful lot about it – I remember looking out the window an awful lot." How could he have impressed anybody, if he was looking out the window?

Or, for example, you're at a management meeting, going through the motions, wishing you were somewhere else. So, part of you is there and part of you thinks you're somewhere else. Then there's another part, that's looking at whether your mask is holding up alright, whether you're performing to the picture that you actually have of yourself. And there's yet another part that's wondering what the others at the meeting think about you. In other words, there is a big piece of you actually looking at the picture that you've created for yourself, as well as a piece of you trying to be there, as well as a piece of you probably wishing you were somewhere else. So, literally – and it's a well worn expression – you're all over the place.

Now, you can't achieve anything in life if you're all over the place. Do you think that's how the high achievers live, how they spend their time or use their mind?

to succeed... JUST LET GO

Doing What You're Doing!

How do you do what you're doing? You use your five senses to engross yourself in this moment. With practice, this becomes second nature (or, actually, first nature!). But there's no point in choosing a crucial moment – like an important meeting, job interview or playing with the kids in the evening – to practise, that's like sending a team out for the Cup Final, telling them that they should use the occasion as a training session. That's why you have your exercises. By practising these, your ability to live in the now is perfected for use in the real world.

For example, you have an important meeting this afternoon, but this time you're going to really be there, you're going to really look at the people sitting opposite you, you're going to hear exactly what they're saying, you're going to feel the emotions that are going on inside you at each moment and you're going to smell and taste the coffee. How different is that from a normal meeting – where you don't really see the other person, you see who you either think you're seing or want to see, based on your previous experience of this person or second-hand knowledge? You normally don't listen to what the other person is saying – you hear what you think they're saying, based on what you think of them and what you think their agenda might be. Consequently, normally your feelings derive from what you think you're seeing and hearing – but you've conned yourself, you're looking through a filter created from thought. My clients, without exception, who actually, really attend and participate in meetings, in the here and now, are often astounded by the results of actually being there. I know, it sounds ridiculous but for years they weren't either where they thought they were or they physically were – they were nowhere, in between!!! Can you guess at the kind of results? Well, first of all, they had meetings where things actually happened, issues were actually sorted out and decisions actually made. They discovered that the agenda that they thought the other person might have somehow wasn't really there when they listened to them. They discovered that their preconceived notion of who the other person was, was wrong – or, where it was right, they were many times more effective at dealing with it. They discovered that, in

The Importance of Now

many cases, the meeting went their way, without them trying – as we know, the one thing that's sure to stop you getting what you want is trying too hard. When they stopped trying and just were there, very often someone else would make the point they'd so badly wanted to make to push their case – but because someone else had made it, it had been accepted. They found that by being there, everyone else seemed to be more focused as well – remember what we said about state of mind being contagious? Above all, they got more done quicker – an achievement that leads to greater happiness, more time and greater clarity of mind – the opposite of the normal vicious circle. Now, it's worth noting that none of these exponents of living in the now were practising it at those meetings – they were actually doing it. You have to train yourself, you have to set your mind each morning, you must do your exercises.

The story is told of Richard Branson, when he was involved in one of his customary dog-fights with British Airways. He has said that whilst he had all these problems going on, he would take each of his problems and "park them to one side", put them "out of my head", and simply focus on what he had to do, there and then. That's what we're talking about – focusing just on the job in hand, whether that job is working through a management meeting, having a wonderful time on a Friday night, playing golf, having a quiet evening with your nearest and dearest, playing with the kids or going for a walk.

When you're in a meeting, wishing you were out playing golf, you can't actually go out and play golf now. The only place you can be at the moment is here, now.

Now – the Only Time Your Subconscious Understands

The importance of the here and now, however, goes way beyond the benefits of doing what you're doing. Your subconscious mind only operates in the present tense. So, if you have an argument with somebody, like my tennis partner John, and you keep re-playing that in your head, it's happening to you again and again now. The programs that we learned about in earlier chapters are all played

to succeed... JUST LET GO

out by your subconscious mind now. The feeling you get when you smell the Sunday roast that brings you back to your childhood, is a feeling you get now. Mess up your now, and you're defeating your subconscious mind's best efforts to bring about the now you want – even if you've already given your subconscious your program, your picture, of your ideal life.

So, if you want to achieve a goal or lifestyle, wanting it, hoping you'll have it or looking forward to it are incomprehensible to the part of your mind that can make it happen for you – your subconscious mind simply doesn't understand anything other than now. Perhaps that's why we were taught, as children, that in the world of the spirit – the subconscious mind – there is no time. For, to your subconscious, there is no past, present or future; there is now, the nows gone by and the nows that are yet to come – only, always the now. How many interviews have you attended where you were asked "Where do you want to be in five years' time?" What bullshit! Five years ago did you plan out, in detail, where you are now? So forget about "I will be...", "I will have...", "I want to be..." – it's all a waste of your conscious energy. The magic piece of you that can bring about the life of your dreams lives now, sees now, creates now – so if you're not here now, not only are you "all over the place", but you're actually reinforcing the barricade that prevents you entering your subconscious mind – beyond the sentry we spoke of in Chapter 3. And, consequently, your life will continue to be not-too-bad.

The Now is Everything

How can you be dissatisfied or unhappy, lonely or worried if you're in the here and now, using your senses to wrap yourself up in the experience of this moment – so wrapped up, that none of your mind is available to think those useless thoughts? It's only thinking and worrying that makes us dissatisfied and it is dissatisfaction and the imaginary consequences of delusory scenarios we concoct through worry that paralyse us from moving beyond the world of not-too-bad. The fact is that through cultivating your ability to operate in

The Importance of Now

clarity of mind, to live in the now, one day you'll wake up and realise you have it all – everything you need for your perfect life, now. Maybe not everything you think you want – but everything you need (for your perfect life). It is the wanting that causes all the heartache – personally, in your relationships, in your work, in your finances. It is the wanting that prevents us being all that we can be – because we're afraid that, in taking risks, we'll move ourselves even further away from the things we want.

When you live in clarity of mind, the wanting stops and the achievement of your goals starts – bringing about your ideal life. These things are no longer wants, they are things your subconscious mind believes you already have – through the pictures you have given it (which we will talk about in detail in Chapter 11). And the best that you can do to bring them all about is do what you're doing now without thought or worry, for these are the distractions that confound normal people – and you're no longer normal.

The point is, you don't have to change job, get a bigger house or drive a bigger car. You don't need to change your clothes, lose that weight; you don't have to change any of those material things at all. You change what is inside – the tiniest of changes in your way of thinking (or not thinking) opens the floodgates of unlimited achievement and abundance.

I've said to people, many of them my friends, that I'm "100 per cent happy" and the reaction of the normal people amongst them never varies – "That's very sad – how could you not want anything else out of life?" Of course, they've missed the key point; I don't want for anything right now, the wanting would only get in the way of the living. And now I know I can achieve all my goals without wanting them so badly as to prevent my achieving them, without me wasting my energy wondering why they haven't happened yet and without wasting my time thinking that my goals might be too big or too unrealistic. None of my mind is idling on these useless distractions – I'm too busy living life to the full in the here and now. It's like skiing – a sport you have to focus on with all of your mind, because your life could depend upon it! You have to do everything as if your life depends on it – because, in reality, it does.

to succeed... JUST LET GO

The Flow

In the now, you experience the flow – it's now a scientifically accepted term and not the cool jargon of the sports-people and movie stars – the natural high we all experience in those clear moments: with good friends, walking through somewhere of great natural beauty, hitting that perfect golf shot, the natural high that is our true mental state, a mental state that's been stifled by useless thought and the programming of society. This is your natural state of mind all of the time – just as the sun shines all of the time, only on miserable rainy days it's obscured by the clouds, but they can't stop it shining. Your clarity of mind exercises are your way of blowing away the clouds of useless thought and programming that have been darkening your blue sky.

When you get into the flow, when you're no longer thinking, just experiencing, the penny actually drops – the gateway to achieving all of your goals, effortlessly, lies in you stopping yourself from thinking, it's as simple as that and as amazingly difficult as that! Try to stop yourself thinking for five minutes. It is very, very hard – but focus on where you are with a clear mind, using your senses to guide you; not only is it simple, it is, perhaps, heaven.

When you're in the flow, things start sorting themselves out for you – normal people call it luck or coincidence, psychologists and scientists call it synchronicity. Have you ever heard the expression "What you don't know can't hurt you"? It's a bit like that. Dave (yes the same sixty-boss Dave) arrived to one of my seminars with the weight of the world on his shoulders. Not only had he his usual list of things to do (and by the time he went home that evening he knew the list would be twice as long), but, on top of all his usual problems, he was renovating a couple of houses as an investment (obviously money wasn't one of his problems!). But the builders had delivered the wrong-sized sinks – "These guys, they delivered the wrong sinks yesterday, what am I going to do about it?" I said, "You're going to do nothing about it at all," and confiscated his mobile phone! That evening there were a number of messages on his phone. 10.00am – they'd replaced the sinks and they were

The Importance of Now

the wrong size as well! 10.20am – the plumber arrived and threw a tantrum. Of course, if Dave got these messages his whole day (possibly his life!) would have been ruined. 2.40pm – the plumber had made a mistake and the new sinks were OK. 4.57pm – the job was finished! He'd done nothing, but think of the amount of energy he would have wasted by checking what was going on, by getting involved, by trying too hard.

Park all your cares and worries and focus on the job in hand. How much more effective would you actually be? (2,000 per cent more effective according to US university research.) What you're wasting your energy worrying about generally sorts itself out – even the big things – and I bet you can't remember what you were worrying about this time, this day, last year (or even last month). You're job is to stay awake. All the great experts of how to use one's mind say this, including the Gospels; stay focused on the job in hand – and the real job in hand is that of living each moment to the full – in the flow, here and now. Consider how effective you are the day that you're due to go on holidays – all the jobs you've put off, but which have to be done before you go, the way you knock each task down, one-at-a-time and the satisfaction you feel from being so effective. That's how you should be every moment of every day. But, of course, effectiveness is not a work thing. Effectiveness is about being effective at every single thing you do – in each here and now.

In the Flow Exercises

The following exercises can be used in pretty much any situation in which you find yourself – I've simply chosen three sample scenarios. The secret in doing them, as in all the clarity of mind exercises, is to use your senses to pay attention to what you're experiencing, as if you're doing it for the first time – in the manner in which a child experiences something new, with no baggage, no preconceptions, no programs or thoughts related to where you are or what you're doing. Familiarity numbs your senses, making your mind lazy and undisciplined, providing it with all the opportunity it needs to

to succeed... JUST LET GO

wander and indulge in the useless thought and distraction that prevents you from being all that you can be.

Exercise 1 – A Business Meeting

1. As you enter the room, consciously look at the colour and décor of the walls, the style of lighting, the table(s) and the way the light reflects off it. Look at the style of the chairs, the colour and type of their upholstery. Feel the way your feet sink into the carpet/squeak on the floor. Consciously pay attention to these physical surroundings, even if you've been in this room many times before.

2. Look – really look – at the other person or people present. Make eye contact (something we often avoid), notice their complexion, the colour of their eyes, the shape, colour and sheen of their hair. Notice the clothes they're wearing (without being judgemental!), the way they sit, their movements and body language. Consciously notice their attributes, as if you'd never seen them before.

3. Feel yourself sitting in your chair, notice how you feel, how it feels to be here, whether it's warm or cool, how the surface of the table feels beneath the palm of your hand, the texture of the material on the seat and arms of the chair. Feel the contours of the pen in your hand. Notice all these feelings, as if you'd never experienced anything quite like them before.

4. Listen, carefully, to each word that is being said – and how it is being said, the speaker's (including your own) tone of voice. Listen to all the extraneous noise, notice the background hum of the air conditioning, the clink of coffee cups, the squeak of chairs – but above all, pay conscious attention to the words that you are hearing, noticing each phrase's meaning (and not ascribing each phrase a

The Importance of Now

predetermined meaning based on your own preconceptions and prejudices).

5. If coffee or tea is served – smell it and taste it!

6. When your mind wanders – and, in particular, when you find yourself sinking into any preconceived ideas about the other attendee(s) – refocus on seeing, feeling and hearing. Repeat steps 1 to 5.

Exercise 2 – Arriving Home

Unfortunately, we're so used to arriving home each evening (and, invariably, dragging the cares of the workday just ended through the front door with us) that we simply don't see the person that might have spent his or her entire day looking forward to this very moment – whether that's a little child, your husband, wife or partner, or your dog.

1. Pay close attention as you walk up to your front door – let the sight of your front door be your key to a wonderful evening.

2. Look clearly at some object – the hall floor covering, wallpaper, coat-stand, hall table, lampshade, etc. – clearly, noticing its colour, size and texture, as if you were seeing it for the first time. Pick a different object every evening. Once you've focused on that object, look at the overall scene before your eyes, the colour, the light, the shade.

3. Consciously greet each of the people – see how they look, notice what they're wearing. If you have young children, listen to the noise that greets you – too often, that noise is shouted down by "Be quiet!", "Shut up, I'm tired", "Go and play, I need to talk to your mother!", "Go and watch the TV, I need a drink!" Listen to and hear what's being said.

to succeed... JUST LET GO

4. Feel what it's like to be greeted and appreciate the feeling of coming home. If you don't like that feeling, that's a useless thought and it's your problem (that quickly becomes everyone else's too). Feel the warmth of an embrace. Feel, smell and taste the warmth of a kiss.

5. Smell the aroma coming from the kitchen (assuming there is one!).

6. Ensure that your coming home is completed – get out of that coat or suit, put your briefcase away – every evening should look and feel like a lazy Sunday afternoon.

7. Once again, remember, use that front door to switch yourself on. Of course, if you were practising your clarity of mind exercise whilst driving home, your entry into a wonderful evening will be completely seamless.

Exercise 3 – Working Out

One of the most effective ways of training your mind is to do so whilst training your body – they really do go hand in hand. Yet, most gyms are full of people half-cycling, half-jogging, half-rowing, whilst the other half of them watches Sky News, MTV or reads a magazine. They might as well be in the pub! If you train your mind whilst training your body, the latter will be more than twice as effective (university research proves this) – so, here goes!

If you can, close your eyes whilst exercising – obviously, this is not possible whilst on the treadmill – it's actually very dangerous! But, in closing your eyes, you can then visualise the muscle you're working expanding, contracting, stretching and straining with each individual movement you make. See the fibres of your muscles stretch, work and firm up, in your mind's eye.

Deliberately focus your feeling on the muscle that is being worked by the particular exercise you're doing. Notice the intense

The Importance of Now

feeling in each of the muscles being worked – to the exclusion of all your other muscles and any other feelings you might have.

Listen to the rhythm of your feet on the treadmill – this can be virtually hypnotic. Listen to the clank of the weights as you move them. Listen to the music in the gym – the beat will often enable you synchronise your movements – but this will be lost on you if you're watching the news! Listen to your own body, to your own heartbeat. Smell your own body odours – lick your lips and taste the perspiration on your upper lip – taste the dryness of your mouth.

Feel the exhilaration and effort of the muscle or muscle group you're working now, to the exclusion of all the other parts of your body and to the exclusion of everything else happening around you. Constantly re-run the sequence of your focus, between visualisation, feeling, hearing, smelling and tasting. Your mental focus on the area of your body that you're exercising will not only focus your effort, but will intensify the workout and generate a greater level of growth hormone. This whole experience is a very inner experience – leading to a much more effective mind-body-spirit workout.

Your Goal for Successful Living

Why enjoy yourself for your two-week-a-year holiday and slave for the other fifty weeks – you can be in the flow twenty-four hours a day, seven days a week, fifty-two weeks a year. The only thing stopping you is you. But practice does make perfect – without your mental workout you can't be mentally fit. Use every opportunity you have – which is every moment of every day – to be here now, using your five senses to be in the flow. You're called upon to rise to be the person you can be, in all your unlimited glory. Your goal must be to be in the flow all of the time.

to succeed... JUST LET GO

Chapter Summary

- You can only be in one place at the moment – here.

- You can only succeed in achieving anything worthwhile if you're actually doing what you're doing here and now.

- If you're 100 per cent doing what you're doing even logic says that you'll be a lot more effective at doing it!

- But there's more to it than that. Now is all your subconscious understands; by focusing in the now, you empower your subconscious, eliminating the barriers of worry, useless thought and programs that normally hinder your subconscious.

- You use your five senses to centre yourself in the here and now – in doing so, you enter the flow, that natural high that is your natural mental state for maximum (or unlimited) effectiveness.

- Use every moment you have to be in that moment – every opportunity to perfect your ability to focus, using your five senses, to be in the here and now.

- In not dissipating your energy through useless thought, you harness your energy so that all the little things you need to happen begin to fall into place effortlessly.

Chapter Nine
Energy and Opportunity

You are composed of energy, as is the entire universe and everything in it. It is how you direct your energy that dictates what you achieve. At their very best, normal people direct their energy within the confines of their programmed belief system – possibly achieving success in one aspect of their lives to the detriment of other aspects and people – achieving what we might consider normal success. That's at best! Normally, however, normal people are all over the place, their mind divided and clogged with useless thought, their energy dissipated in a multitude of directions. The exceptional success that is their birthright is not only beyond their grasp but many levels beyond their comprehension. And yet, in clearing your mind and thereby focusing your energy, you have at your disposal the very stuff of which our universe is made – and to which our universe responds.

Energy and Matter

In the information age, we all know about cells, DNA and atoms – there are even books on quantum physics finding their way to bestsellers' lists! Science is now providing logical proof, for our well-programmed logical minds, that our universe is a mystical place over which even our thoughts have an influence. You are composed of atoms. Each atom contains a nucleus around which electrons orbit – we've all seen the diagrams! But consider the amount of

to succeed... JUST LET GO

empty space in each of us; if the central nucleus of each cell were the size of a grain of salt, each orbiting electron would be hundreds of feet away from it. We – and all seemingly solid material – are energy or light which vibrates to produce, in the first instance, our physical form.

But you are only too well aware that you do not stop at the outer bounds of your physical body; your energy field stretches many feet in all directions from you. Some call this your aura – an expression which turns many people off straight away – science would prefer to call it the outer extremities of your subtle energy. Leading universities worldwide now have chairs or departments of subtle energy and advances in photography have enabled the magnetic field created by your subtle energy to be photographed. Your subtle energy is in direct communication with others' subtle energy and with cosmic energy. These are scientific facts – and science is beginning to discover the most amazing facts about your energy and its abilities to communicate and influence your environment and surroundings.

Research has demonstrated that even our observing external phenomena changes external events; laboratory experiment has proved that a kettle observed whilst boiling, comes to the boil more slowly! Recent US university research has established the mind's ability to influence the computer selection of random numbers. And scientists at CERN, the European Centre for Nuclear Research at Geneva, have, using the world's largest scientific instrument, the 27km long particle accelerator, gone a long way to proving what was known as "Bell's Theorem", put forward by the Irish quantum physicist, John Bell, in the 1970s. Simply put, it states that two pieces of a particle, once connected, are always connected. At CERN, an atomic particle was split in two, the pieces sent in opposite directions. When one piece was spun, its twin spun, in the same direction, simultaneously. So it is throughout the universe. And we are all part of the universe – originally emerging from nothing other than energy.

Energy And Opportunity

Children and Energy

You should not be surprised, given your new understanding of the manner in which a child's mind is impressionable owing to its clear state, that young children are acutely aware of our energy. Your young child knows when you're really playing with him or her in the evening and when you're simply going through the motions – whether you're all there or not is immediately evident to a young child – they can see through you! At a more fundamental level, young children are fully tuned into the energy dimension of our lives, all of the time – they can see your energy field.

At one of my seminars I said to the guys, "When we go for our coffee, if there are any young kids around, just notice how they look at you"; we had just done one of the clarity of mind exercises, so our energy was pretty high. Aidan, the biggest cynic of all, came up to me afterwards. "I was standing in the queue and there was this little kid in a buggy, staring up at me," he said. "He was looking up above my forehead." The child in the pushchair was impressed or mesmerised by Aidan's energy and, in all probability, was looking at the colour of his energy field. This led to me asking my youngest daughter what she could see when she looked at our faces. Sarah replied that we all had a glow around our heads like the halos in holy pictures, that our second daughter's "halo" was gold, our eldest son's was "creamy" and that my own and my wife's were "darker". The sad fact is that, as we grow beyond our formative years, thought and programming suppresses our vital energy, to the point where normal people not only don't know that it exists but scoff at the idea of its existence as fanciful or some New Age nonsense. Yet, that it's there and visible is a scientific fact.

The Real World

What does all this mean in practice? First of all, it means that there's more to you than meets the eye! Have you ever been in a shop when the shop assistant simply gets too close to you? Or in a pub when an

to succeed... JUST LET GO

acquaintance "invades your space"? Ever noticed someone stepping into your field of subtle energy? You notice it frequently, at an instinctive level. Do you have days when you're full of energy – days when you, quite literally, feel more alive? Again, you instinctively know that feeling – and it's all to do with the state of mind you're in, which we discussed in Chapter 7. Have you ever been with someone who drains you, in whose presence you become exhausted? You instinctively recognise the feeling when someone is literally feeding off your energy, stealing it from you.

The real world – not your version of reality as we've discussed through many of the early chapters of this book – is an energetic one. But one that normal people cannot experience, because their vital energy is stopped in its tracks by useless thought and mind-numbing programming. The real world is experienced by your cleared mind – it is a world that responds to the beliefs of your uncluttered subconscious mind.

Your Vital Energy

There is a wonderful irony that the very science that set out to explain God in rational terms is now confirming what spiritualists and mystics have known, through tradition, for millennia: Eastern mysticism that focuses on your chi – your vital energy; acupuncture that seeks to prevent illness through maintaining the clear passage of your vital energy through your body – and cures illness caused by thoughts, worry and stress blocking those energy channels; meditation that seeks to align your vibration in the seven key energy centres in your body – your chakras.

You know that stress disrupts the regularity of your heartbeat. You also know that stress can cause stomach ulcers. Stress is a medically accepted cause of impotence and infertility. And television commercials for decades have talked of a "tense, nervous headache". Of course, you also know that stress and tension are a figment of a cluttered mind, overwhelmed by useless thought and even more useless programs.

Energy And Opportunity

So, it is vital that you compose yourself, using the exercises in this book, and align your energy. Again, just like your instinctive knowledge of your subtle energy, you already instinctively know when your vibrations are wrong – when one part of your body is out of kilter with the rest of you or of what's going on around you. You have dozens of "figures of speech" to describe your feelings of a block in your vital energy – from the "lump in your throat", to that sick feeling "in the pit of your stomach" – from that "quiver in your voice", to "the shakes" you get in your hand. Something – in your gut – doesn't feel quite right. Your vital energy is out of synch.

Tuning In

In clearing your mind, you tune in to your own vital energy and the vital energy of everyone and everything around you – with important consequences. First of all, and very logically, when you clear your mind, you "set your mind at ease". This in itself enables you focus your energy on the job in hand – we've already talked about this, though not in terms of your vital energy. Secondly, with your energy unimpeded, you are really there with and for whoever you're with at this moment – to achieve anything in terms of any relationship (whether that's your loved one, your boss, your colleagues, or the guy to whom you're trying to sell double-glazing) you must be all here because your subconscious communication is more profound and has a deeper impact than your talking or your mere physical presence. Thirdly – well, let's deal with secondly first!!

I've already mentioned people who drain you – they're so negative that they need to go in search of someone else's energy to replenish their depleted resources – they're the energy snatchers. I used to share an office with Bernard. We always had a laugh, were full of "get up and go" and always got the job done in double-quick time. Yet, some evenings, we'd find ourselves flat – almost lifeless – as we'd make our way to the car park and we began to wonder why. Having considered it, we discovered that we felt low on days we'd been to lunch with a certain Bob. Think of the most bubbly

to succeed... JUST LET GO

person you know – he or she would be bored to tears by Bob. Twenty minutes with Bob and you'd be emotionally drained – you'd be only fit for the bed!

In the last paragraph, you will find nine phrases in everyday use to describe the state of your energy, good or bad – so you know what I'm talking about, you feel it every day, instinctively. You know there are people who exhaust you. You also know that there are people who are full of life, full of beans, a joy to be with, people who raise the energy level wherever they go. You'd say that these people have charisma or they have presence – meaning, of course, that they are present, here and now – all their energy is here at their disposal, now, and you can feel it.

You send out and receive subconscious signals all of the time – it is your most important means of communication. For example, on meeting someone for the first time, you form your first impression of that person in approximately four seconds – before they open their mouth to introduce themselves! This impression – how your subconscious mind is impressed – is based on that person's energy level, whether they are all there or all over the place! You communicate at this subconscious level all of the time. How effective you are is based on whether you're here in spirit (rather than just here bodily) with an open mind, with the full resources of your vital energy freely available to you and those around you. And as you already know, your clear state of mind is contagious – you will draw those you're with into your higher energy level, just like the person with charisma or presence. Consider the consequences from a personal relationship perspective – or from a business standpoint.

If, for example, you're in sales and, right now, you're way ahead of your target – the common expression would be that you're on a roll (in the flow!) – you go to meet each new customer simply knowing how good you are. This belief self-transmits subconsciously, your customer is *impressed* by this and is immediately more likely to buy – you might as well have "super sales person" tattooed on your forehead!! Anyone involved in sales knows that the guy most likely to have new sales fall into his lap is the guy who's already way ahead. And we all know the converse holds true too – the guy who's behind

Energy And Opportunity

target finds the whole process a struggle. If you're a sales person, down on your luck, meeting a potential new customer, how can you impress them if you haven't managed to impress yourself?

A recent university study shows that if you're trying to impress somebody – that could be selling to someone, making a presentation, chatting up the blonde at the bar, chatting to your partner at home – the impact that you have on that person is largely the result of non-verbal communication. Fifty-six per cent of the impact results from your body language, 38 per cent from your tone of voice and only 6 per cent from what you actually say. When you're talking to someone, how conscious are you of your body language or tone of voice? The answer is – not at all – these are subconscious things, like the reactions we spoke of all the way back in Chapter 1! But, as I've already said, when you're operating in the now, with a clear mind, all of your energy is available to impress the person with whom you're otherwise trying to communicate.

But there's even more to it than that!

Opportunity

If you are fully focused, fully energised and thereby fully and subconsciously communicating with those around you, people who might otherwise not even notice you will find you attractive – in other words, they will be aware of your presence (I'm not simply referring to attractiveness in the sexual sense, but I don't exclude it either) – they will be drawn to you, just as you feel the *presence* of someone with charisma entering your *presence*. And if the vast majority of your impressive communication is non-verbal, the real communication between you and someone else may well have started long before you become consciously aware of it. In short, if you're all there, you will find yourself meeting people and talking to people who you might otherwise be completely unaware of – you may end up bumping into people who change your life.

Let's take a very simple example. Many years ago, whilst studying this very subject in the Swiss ski resort of Villars – all the non-exotic

to succeed... JUST LET GO

locations were unavailable! – both I and my colleagues noticed how our higher level of presence could be put to a very practical advantage. Each evening, we would mingle with the tourists in the local bars. But, for me, there would normally be a problem – I become invisible when I stand at a bar! Barmen clean glasses, re-arrange bottles, shine the pumps – do anything other than serve me. With our energy high, things were different. In Villars, I would take my place at the bar, behind bronzed six-foot-six guys who'd been waiting ten minutes – and the barman always served me first. The minute I walked in, he'd notice me. The other wonderful thing I found was that all the attractive women would look me straight in the eye! When you're all there, you connect with everyone else at a different, more fundamental, more impressive level. When you're all there – your vital energy fully available for all to notice – both you and those around you are far more likely to take note of what's happening. This may sound obvious, but it's completely at odds with how normal people automatically behave. Normal people are too concerned about who's doing what to them, how they look or what other people think of them, whether they'll have enough money at the end of the month to keep the bank manager happy or whether their neighbours have a bigger car or house than them. This is the crap that feeds off normal people's energy, sucking them dry of their vital energy, leaving them blind and oblivious to what's really happening around them, how many opportunities are passing them by – because they're simply not looking, they're simply not all there. Opportunity's knuckles are red and bruised from knocking on your door – the lights have been on, but no-one's been home!

Yet, with your energy completely free – by your having *cleared your mind* and focused in the now – you're awake and alive to every opportunity that comes your way. You know, only too well, the expression "the right man, in the right place at the right time" and how seldom it happens in your normal life. In the *ab*normal world of the high achiever, this happens with great regularity – with what normal people would describe as unbelievable results. Normal people call it coincidence – or, even worse, chance. But when your subconscious mind has been set to achieve your *true goals* and when it

Energy And Opportunity

has then been left to set about their achievement free from thought and worry, your subconscious energy notices these coincidences as they occur – because you're fully there to notice!

Synchronicity

This is the phenomenon that Karl Jung described as synchronicity and that so many after him have worked on and written about at length. It is the phenomenon of your subconscious energy bringing about the circumstances that you need at just the right time to enable you progress towards the goals to which you have set your subconscious. Much scientific research has already established all the elements that bring about synchronicity – we've discussed this already. But, then again, you know about synchronicity already too. Consider your current position in life, whatever that might be, or however it might appear to you. You have met a person or people, at particular crossroads in your life, who have set your life off in a particular direction, for better or for worse. Consider the number of times you have needed to get a piece of advice or information, and you simply happened by it, just at the right time. How often has someone popped into your head – and that same person phones you, or you bump into them? The more aware you are, the freer your mind is, the more you notice these events, the more you're present to grasp the opportunity that those events might present.

For example, Gerry spent a week on a career development program a couple of years ago, during the course of which he decided that he would leave his then current job and set up a software business – it was a dream of his, the fact that he knew little of computers and less of the actual manufacture of software had little bearing on his single-mindedness! On his return to the office, his desk was piled high with a week's mail, mostly garbage. However, sitting atop the pile was an internal memo from the Personnel Division offering interest-free staff loans to those wishing to buy a PC – and that's how he bought his first computer. Within twenty-four hours, he had bought just the manuals he needed to get

to succeed... JUST LET GO

himself going in computer programming. Whilst walking through a bookshop – on his way to the toilet! – he knocked down a pile of computer programming books for beginners with his briefcase! Within six months, his then employer had made him a very lucrative offer of voluntary redundancy and he had bumped into an old acquaintance who explained to him the most pressing needs of that business sector for a particular piece of software that was not then available. Within two years, Gerry's company was the leading provider in its field in its home market. It was all effortless (that's not to say that there was no hard work involved – but work is only hard in the mind of the doer!).

Sam worked as a personal tax consultant and was bored to the point of suicide with his work. He would take two-hour lunches to avoid the misery of having to go back to the office. He decided to set up his own tax consultancy – something that would probably have further depressed him, for it wasn't his ideal solution but it was the only one he could think of – and was on his way back from the printer with his new headed paper, when he wandered into a church, something that was entirely out of character. He found himself drawn to the confessional, went in, closed the door, knelt down and had no idea what to say or do next! The grille between him and the priest slid open and an elderly man the opposite side said to him: "You're having grave trouble in your work at present! – Know that Life is looking after you." In a daze, Sam returned to his office. Ten minutes later, his phone rang. An acquaintance with whom he had worked many years previously, asked him if he would like to attend an interview for a job in a large financial services company, developing tax-based products. Three weeks later, Sam was on his way to a new and fruitful career.

Tom needed cash for an investment opportunity – immediately! He was well versed in the manner in which synchronicity works, he simply knew that everything would be alright, so he booked his airline tickets for a month-long holiday to Australia. When he did this, he needed a six-figure sum and had no way of getting it! Three days before he flew out, Greg called him and asked him if he could organise, through some of his wealthy clients, a loan for

Energy And Opportunity

a new business venture – and offered him a finder's fee of exactly the amount he needed. Tom flew out to Australia having finalised his investment.

When your energy channels are open, you attract all the good things to you – or, to put it another way, if in clearing your mind, you put living first, everything you need will fall into place. In a passage in the Bible, read and completely ignored by millions of believers, it quite clearly says that you should not waste your energy worrying, you should not consume your mental energy on concerning yourself with whether you'll have sufficient wealth, but you should simply open your mind, put Life first, and everything you need for your perfect life will simply be given to you. I've met only half-a-dozen people in my life who believe this to the point of their living their lives accordingly – we'll discuss some of them in the next chapter. But, at this point, it is vital that you understand that in clearing your mind, your mental energy is fully available to seize each opportunity and, in doing so, seize the moment.

Universal Energy

Everything is composed of energy. Science has determined that particles once linked are linked forever – remember Bell's Theorem. All matter originated in what scientists call the Big Bang. We are all linked, all part of a whole that is infinitely more powerful than any single part. We are all linked to each other – call it subconsciously or by way of our subtle energy, the different terms are mere semantics – we are all energetic, spiritual beings in an energetic, spiritual world and universe. But thought suppresses our energy to the point that normal people are blissfully unaware of their source of universal energy. Awareness of that energy is everything. This awareness is awakened and maintained by awareness of the moment, using your five senses, without programming or thought in all its horrible forms – judgement, doubt, fear, anxiety, stress – the list is an endless list that adequately describes the problems of our lives and of our world. All problems stop when thought stops. Awareness

to succeed... JUST LET GO

begins when thought stops, your connection to universal energy is re-kindled when awareness starts.

Every word you speak counts, every action you take counts. They define who you are at this moment and whether you're aware or dead to the world. Every thought you nurture counts. When you clear your mind, your connection to universal energy brings about what you need to happen, to bring about your perfect life. It is that simple – it is so simple that the normal logical mind has immense problems accepting it – it is only in letting go that you experience the reality that this is how your world works. Do remember that, whether you accept this fact or not, this is the way your world already works – a *not-too-bad* expectation brings forth a not-too-bad life, as we discussed earlier. The fact is that muddled minds have created a muddled world.

You can change this for you – the choice is yours.

Freeing Your Energy – Your Awareness

When you do any of the exercises in this book, you free your energy, and the more you free your energy, the more you provide yourself with the ability to be here, now.

Your exceptional success depends solely on your ability to focus. Not focus on what you want out of life, it depends solely on your ability to focus now, with a clear mind. You don't have to work hard to be a success. Effort, stress and worry waste your energy. You don't even have to say no to effort, stress and worry. It's easier than that, you simply *refocus*, using your five senses on now, clearing your mind and freeing your energy to tune you into the flow and plug you into the universal energy of which we are all a part and to which it is our natural state to be connected. Then you can make your energy freely available to others.

Energy And Opportunity

Chapter Summary

- You are energy – everyone and everything is energy. Your own personal energy field stretches beyond the confines of your physical body. Children are constantly aware of this subtle energy.

- All matter is atomically linked. Science is now determining the scientific facts underlying mysticism and spirituality.

- The real world – very different from normal people's versions of reality – responds to your energy.

- You already understand this through your experience of subconscious communication – many times more powerful than verbal communication.

- In thought, your energy is suppressed and you are unable to tune in to the opportunities that life offers you.

- In awareness, your are at tuned to the coincidences or synchronicity that effortlessly lead you to your perfect life.

- Your success in living a full life depends on your ability to clear your mind and become aware, focusing only in the present moment, without thought or worry.

Chapter Ten
Let Go

A good friend, Harold, whilst living through the horrors of the virtual dictatorship of Robert Mugabe's Zimbabwe, told me this story one evening, from his home in Harare where he was trying to maintain some semblance of normal living with his wife and two young children.

A climber set out one morning, intent on conquering a difficult peak in one day's climbing. The morning sun illuminated the mountain like a stage set as he began his climb, full of enthusiasm and energy. By noon, with the sun at its full height, he had made the progress he had planned and sat, basking in the sunshine enjoying a nourishing lunch. He pressed ahead, labouring harder as the climb steepened and as the late afternoon sun slanted across the sky and cast its long shadows over his path. The cool early evening air chilled against the perspiration that beaded on his forehead. Night fell but his determination kept him going, his way lit by a miner's headlamp. Cloud cover gave a moonless night and as his lamp's battery failed the darkness enveloped him as he stumbled ever forward and upward. Lost in the darkness, he lost his footing, stumbling off a ledge into the open blindness of the fresh air. Freefalling through the air, the chill wind became a gale, icing his cheeks. With a body wrenching jerk, his support rope snapped him to a halt, dangling him in black midair like a ball hanging helplessly from a Christmas tree. In shock and silence he swung to and fro, like a pendulum.

In fear and desperation, he moaned, "God! Help me."

to succeed... JUST LET GO

A voice from the darkness casually answered, "Do you really believe I could do that?"

Startled, the climber stammered, "Yes! I do... I do believe."

The voice replied, "Then let go the rope!" But the climber's faith didn't stretch that far. As the sun rose on a beautiful fresh, clear morning, the frozen body of a dead climber was discovered by a hiker – less than two feet from the ground.

How many of us are completely unaware of just how close the power of universal energy is to each of us? And how fiercely do we cling to our safety ropes? For example, I recently asked one of my clients, Jack, if he could count how many business opportunities he had let slip because he couldn't do without his safety net – the wrap-round comfort of working for a large corporation. Jack conceded that too many opportunities had gone a-begging.

Are You Attached to Your Supports?

Normal people think they know best – normal people will always opt for the comfort of the soothers they've built into their sorry little lives. And normal people are not uncomfortable enough to take what they perceive to be the life-threatening risk of letting go the rope. And yet, how many normal people have heard that well-worn phrase "Let go – Let God!" How many normal people buy vast quantities of books (this one included) that carry this very simple message, yet will not take the leap? Isn't it horrible that only the lucky few who have had the privilege of near-death experience are prepared to let Life look after them, rather than place their trust in the pensionable job, the company car, the stock market or the big house. In one of Life's most amazing ironies, if you do let go, universal energy, which we discussed in Chapter 9, actually provides you with all the supports you need and more – much more than your own man-made supports could ever provide.

Letting go is what every spiritualist and mystic has advocated across the ages – some may call it non-attachment, others detachment, whilst still others have said that the one thing that will stop you

Let Go

getting what you want is trying too hard; others still have said that if you want something really badly, then you're in big trouble – what happens if you don't get it? It all boils down to the same thing – and it's exactly the same as the solution to a problem coming to you when you're not wasting your energy thinking about it – if you put Life first, Life looks after you. You can call Life "God", "universal energy", "the Kingdom of God", call it what suits you best, but the fundamental truth doesn't change. Detach yourself from the wants that consume your energy, free your mind and everything you need will start to flow.

I haven't yet met anyone that this idea doesn't appeal to – and there are millions of people across the globe who listen to these or similar words in their place of worship at least once a year. And almost no-one is bold enough to take the simple step – of letting go. To borrow a well-worn phrase, "Oh, ye of little faith!"

Comfort and Desperation

Not-too-bad means just that – normal people are not uncomfortable enough to let go. Normal people are prepared to decorate the padded prison cell of their programmed lives to make their imprisonment by their thoughts and programs as painless as possible – normal people are not prepared to break free. They are afraid that, in breaking free they may discover their own power, might have to take responsibility – "Our deepest fear is that we are powerful beyond reason." Are you afraid of your own Light?

It could be disheartening – but I'm not easily disheartened – to come to the conclusion that normal people (and remember that includes pretty much all of us) need to become desperate before they'll do anything about their predicament. And it is amazing how much suffering will be endured and how adaptable normal people are to their suffering before they are prepared to take the simple step of letting go. In all my years working with my many clients, I believe I have only come across two cases of complete surrender to Life – in the positive sense of surrender, that of letting Life give them

to succeed... JUST LET GO

what they most need to bring about their perfect life. In both cases, a low point of abject desperation had first to be reached and in both cases, both partners in each relationship took the leap together – the phrase "where two or more…" springs to mind.

Fred and Valerie

For many years, Fred spent his career in the corporate world, working his way up the corporate ladder to a point where he had an extremely substantial safety net. But something kept niggling at Fred – an inner desire to break free and work for himself. Using the many logical powers that he possessed, he and his wife decided that their way to material wealth lay in computer software – after all, whiz kids with no sound business experience (like Fred had) were becoming software millionaires. Fred gave up all his corporate safety nets in the pursuit of this dream – and after a couple of years hard work, Fred had a fledgling software business, making its mark in its home market and attracting the attention of potential investors. The millions that Fred and Valerie dreamed of were within reach.

They took on a couple of serious venture capitalists who, within months, began an internal struggle to gain control of Fred's business. This coincided with the collapse of the "Dot Com" phenomenon and a slump in the financial markets at which Fred's software was aimed. The unscrupulous venture capitalists made their move, took Board decisions behind Fred's back, diverted funds and, effectively, stole Fred's business, leaving Fred with a mountain of debt. At an all-time low, Fred and Valerie reckoned that the most important thing they possessed was each other and their children. Forced to sell their house, they moved to their holiday home – an idyllic spot looking out over the Mediterranean – put their children into local school, without a single word of the local language, and set about living their lives rather than "working for a living".

By the strangest of coincidences, Fred, on arranging to meet an old friend, was introduced to a specialist investment manager who was offering returns that were too good to be true. Without

Let Go

thinking about it, Fred and Valerie decided to invest most of the money they had made from the sale of their home – the greater part of the money they had left. Fred spent his first summer abroad playing with his children. His children told him they had had the best summer ever, a far cry from not seeing their father as he worked eighteen-hour days, seven days a week building up a business to which he had become so attached he hadn't been aware enough to see the bad guys coming! Fred and Valerie don't work for their living now – they just live off their investments, have bought a new home and are devoting their time to talking to other people – trying to wake other normal people up to the error of their ways.

Fred and Valerie had lost almost everything that they'd been attached to and in doing so realised the fatal disease that attachment is. What if they had gained the whole software world and lost their souls in the process. Their children certainly hadn't seen the sense in striving, with such effort, for such an empty goal, a goal which detracted from their quality of life, rather than adding to it. Some will say, you've got to lose your life to find it – and maybe you have – but I hope it's not true. Otherwise, the world of normal people will not only never awaken – but will destroy itself as surely as the Roman Empire fell, as surely as Atlantis before it.

Fred and Valerie woke up from the depths of desperation and said to themselves – let's do what feels right (without knowing why it felt right), and see what happens. They let go – let go of their attachment to material success, let go of their safety nets, let go of their programmed belief that they'd learned through seeing other people become software millionaires, let go of their attachment to their big cars (and many of their "friends" thought the worse of them for it!), simply let go. Now, living in a beautiful place, Fred playing his dearly loved golf, each of them spending loads of time with their children, Fred and Valerie are making the money that they'd previously only dreamed of – financial independence came to them when they'd stopped valuing it as the fool's gold that it is!

to succeed... JUST LET GO

Rico and Diane

Rico and Diane lived comfortably – she had had a meteoric rise through the ranks of a major company, he ran a successful shop. The only problem was they never saw each other or their only child – they were too busy working to make a living! Diane travelled extensively in her job and Rico worked an eighteen-hour day, six days a week, sometimes seven. He was convinced that his shop couldn't run without him. The odd time they were at home together, they almost had to introduce themselves to each other and their young daughter!! Given their circumstances, it was rather odd that they were so obsessed with having another child – an endeavour in which they had repeatedly failed with traumatic results.

Things went from bad to worse – Rico began to suffer from chronic back pain and was admitted to hospital for an emergency operation to remove a number of fused spinal discs that, had they not been operated upon, would have led to certain paralysis. Even from his hospital bed, Rico was on his mobile phone to his suppliers and staff, making sure that the shop didn't lack his special touch. Following the operation, Rico lost some feeling in both his legs and the surgeons were unsure if he'd be able to walk again. After a couple of days spent lying practically motionless in his hospital bed, Rico began to wonder at the lunacy of his situation; he hadn't been able to phone the shop or his suppliers for a couple of days, yet the shop ran smoothly without him! What had he been doing for the last fifteen years? And, at what price? Diane was wondering exactly the same thing as she re-arranged her action-packed days to realise that she got more done in less time – and saw more of their daughter. That evening, as she walked into Rico's hospital ward, they looked each other in the eye and, at the same time, said to each other "I think we should sell the shop." And before Rico left hospital, the deal was in motion, the estate agent appointed and the property advertised.

Rico and Diane didn't stop there – Diane took the option to work a three-day week, Rico was back on his feet many times quicker than any of those treating him had foreseen, Diane became pregnant and

Let Go

the shop sold for a record price. I asked Rico what he planned to do next – his answer "I don't know, let's see what Life comes up with!"

Nowadays, Rico spends his days looking after their three children, playing golf, working out in the gym, and driving the four-wheel-drive that he'd visualised. Diane has just got a new job, working at the pace and hours that suits them both. And they've been on long summer holidays for the last couple of years – something that Rico's shop had never allowed! To quote from a well-known film, "It took a coma to wake me up!"

How Uncomfortable is Worse Than Not-too-bad?

It does concern me that people need to suffer that near-death experience or that coma-to-wake-me-up to actually wake up. Reading this book may lead to your waking up – but will not cause it to happen. Only you can make that decision. But normal people have immense reserves of determination to put up with almost any level of pain and suffering – and, throughout history, we have lauded that resourcefulness and staying power. Not-too-bad can become very bad indeed for most normal people before they are prepared to cry halt and do something different to change their circumstances.

Jack, my client, who is a self-confessed hanger-on to his safety net, is just as concerned as I am. He wants to get off his treadmill and start living life to the full – it's just that he isn't uncomfortable enough, he can't make himself desperate enough. And yet, he knows how Life looks after him when he clears his mind, he's experienced the magic (his words, not mine) of how he came by his latest job, just when he needed it. He's noticed the coincidences in his life as they happen and profited greatly and immediately from the results. For example, Jack was working in an organisation that, he believed, wasn't going anywhere. Although this was his gut feeling, he contented himself with his comfortable lifestyle – the car, the club subscription, the lavish expense account (all the things he knew would vanish if his employer vanished!) – and could not shake himself from his not-too-bad slumber. His company was organising

to succeed... JUST LET GO

corporate entertainment, lunch and tickets to a rugby international, and he found himself with a ticket to spare after a client pulled out at the last minute. His boss gave the ticket to a friend who, sitting beside Jack in the stand, offered him a new job during the match. The new job was more than a considerable improvement on his existing one, which vanished anyway when the shareholders decided to sell up. Having experienced that level of synchronicity, of universal energy coming to the rescue, Jack still feels he's not desperate enough to let go – and this is what concerns me.

Detachment

We let go when we detach ourselves from all our preconceived notions of what makes us – or will make us – happy. You know the kind of notions I mean. "I'm secure in this job – I know where my salary is coming from for the foreseeable future" – and there are many who said this who know just how wrong that feeling of security can be! "I'll be happy when I've moved to that house" – or "when I get that car" – or "when I lose that weight". "I'm happy with you" – "I'd be lost without you" – "I'm happy in my work". All this so-called happiness depends on something or someone else and in giving someone or something else the power to make you happy, so you give them the power to make you unhappy. Your happiness cannot depend on anything just as your life cannot depend on anything external. You have to detach yourself from your dependencies – you must let go. In becoming detached, you open up the treasure box of universal energy and, as we've seen, real magic really happens.

But how can you be detached – how can you let go? The route to success, as defined in the next chapter, starts with a clear mind. All your obsessions, your dependencies, your needs and wants, your perceived safety nets and your falsely founded belief that financial security equals security are simply programs filling your mind with thoughts so useless as to lead you in exactly the opposite direction to that in which you'll find real success, forcing you to continually try harder to achieve those goals on which you think your happiness

Let Go

depends. And trying too hard means you won't achieve those goals – even the concept of trying too hard means that you think you must do so because you inherently believe you'll fail.

Clarity of Mind

When you experience clarity of mind, you are – by definition – detached; you have let go, even if only for the time you've taken to practise a clarity of mind exercise. Would that your mind could be that clear most of the time (because thoughts pop into your mind, I don't say "all of the time"). I do not mean that you have let go of control, you have let go of all the nonsense that normal people cling to – to continually fool themselves that they are in control. In letting go, you take control of your own mind – free from thought, free from limiting programs.

When you let go, you set your inner subconscious power free to bring about and notice the coincidences that will lead you onward and upward to your perfect life. Clarity of mind is the only way to achieve this letting go.

The Practicality

Let's be practical about this. I am not suggesting that you don't take practical steps in your daily life, for example to ensure your mortgage will be paid at the end of the month. But I am proposing that you stop worrying about it. I am proposing that you stop working to earn a living and start living – these are not nice words to make you feel good, this means that you work for the sake of working, in a clear state of mind – and just see how effective you become. If you don't like the work you're doing, keep your mind clear and the work that really suits you will find you – just as it did for Jack.

to succeed... JUST LET GO

I am proposing that you clear your mind of all useless thoughts and worries – immediately. You know for a fact, in your heart and soul, that all worrying is, at very best, completely useless and, at worst, is best left unsaid. You know for a fact that all useless thoughts distract you, slow you down, take your mind off what you're supposed to be doing now.

I am proposing that you detach yourself from any specific goals you have and on which you believe your happiness depends. Given your unlimited potential which springs from your subconscious inner strength, you know that your own goals – expressed as they are from your limited view of the world and the lack of availability of all the relevant facts – are not only less than what you can be but that often, in the past, their achievement still left you wanting something more.

I propose that you stop thinking that you know best how to achieve success. You know for a fact that the coincidences that brought you to where you are prove that you don't know best and that structured logical planning never gets carried out and, therefore, does not work.

I propose that you let go of all the muddle in your mind, all the automatic reactions that come from your programs and start seeing, feeling, hearing, smelling and tasting where you are now. I propose that you come to your senses – that you become carefree which is the exact opposite of careless.

In your daily life that means that you live each moment – seeing, feeling, hearing, smelling and tasting where you are and what you're actually doing (not what you think you're doing or what you'd like to be doing).

The Consequences of Letting Go

Put Life – your life – first and everything else falls into place. Sacred scripture of many traditions and the learned writings of mystics throughout the ages all say this, yet there are few who take it seriously.

Let Go

For a start, if you let go of all your cares, worries, concerns, useless thoughts, fears and programs, consider the weight that will be immediately lifted off your shoulders. Consider how much more effective you'll be. Consider how much livelier and happier you'll be each evening playing with your children, really being with your husband, wife or partner, rather than re-living the stresses and strains of a not-too-bad day. I've known many clients who have, as a result of letting go of their muddle, let go of some of the habits they'd formed to counteract that muddle – drinking to excess is the one that immediately springs to mind.

But that's only for starters. Consider how your free mind will be available to spot the coincidences and to really communicate subconsciously to bring about those coincidences. Consider how freely available your energy will be and how that energy will be tuned into universal energy – and consider the unlimited consequences.

Consider the fact – not the possibility – that you will live life and live it to the full. And then consider the alternative – there is no choice.

Chapter Summary

- You are attached to the supports that you believe provide security and happiness – or, at least, not-too-badness.

- You worry that one or more of these supports might be removed and you strive to maintain them, believing that your relative comfort is better than not knowing what will provide your security in the future.

- But you do not know what provides your security – it is not financial security (which can fail at any time) – nor do you know how great your life might be.

- Not-too-bad is not bad enough for normal people to let go of their obsessions and dependencies – normally only desperation leads to letting go.

to succeed... JUST LET GO

- Yet, the consequences of letting go are unlimited – your carefree mind is fully available to you to bring about the life you're entitled to.

- You let go by maintaining clarity of mind and coming to your senses.

Chapter Eleven
Your Goals

It is amazing the number of business people who come to me having sorted out a strategy for their business, but who have no strategy for themselves. They don't know what they want out of life, but they do know that what they have at the moment isn't it. John called me the day he became National Sales Manager for a large company and said, "All I ever wanted was to be the National Sales Manager. And today, I've made it, I am the National Sales Manager and it's doing absolutely nothing for me – I've got to the top of the mountain and I don't like the view."

Consider for a moment those who are considered successful by normal standards. Most are spectacularly successful in one aspect of their lives – often to the detriment of the rest of their lives and the lives of those around them. Without naming names, consider how many business people have achieved their success at the direct expense of others. Consider the so-called successful people who are on their third or fourth marriage or relationship – and consider the programs they're passing on to their children. Consider the super successful people who are on drugs, just coming off drugs – or achieved their success with the help of drugs! Certainly, these pillars of success are single-minded, often to the extent that they are completely oblivious to the damage they are inflicting on others and on themselves.

But is that success? Certainly, knowing what you now know, you can have that kind of success effortlessly – but, be careful what you wish for, you might just get it!! No – in your clear state of mind, you

to succeed... JUST LET GO

feel that there is more to success than how it is defined by normal people. You feel that success should be in all aspects of your life – and on your terms, based on your own definition of success. After all, if you're a success based on someone else's definition, then you're back into the programmed half-life of "What does he think of me?" – or worse, "What does he think of my new car?"

Defining Success

Success is effortless happiness, contentment, peace and plenty in every aspect of your life. Success is living life to the full now. We can all achieve this success – but only if we are clear in our minds.

Your perceived lack of success, or your imagined stress or distress, unhappiness or even fear are the product of nothing other than your mind not being clear. But, this is not to say that success (as I've defined it above) equates to wandering around in some sort of state of mental bliss – where's the practicality of that? What would be the point of that and what good would you be to others in that state of mind?

When I say success, I mean success – including, but not limited to, the trappings of success that normal people would recognise. Read my definition above again. Could it be possible, is it possible, are there people achieving that success at present? The answer to all those questions is a resounding "Yes".

There are many consequences of this type of success – but I can only describe these consequences; you'll know actual success for yourself only when you experience it, I can't describe your feeling of success for you! These consequences include: being carefree (not careless); getting what needs to be done completed in double-quick time; coming across who and what you need at just the right moment; doing what you most enjoy most of the time; doing what you least enjoy effectively – by simply doing it; having incredible personal relationships; spending more time doing nothing – really relaxing; good health and fitness; having abundance in every aspect of your life.

Your Goals

There are things you discard in living this way – and, believe it or not, most of my clients are afraid to let these things go! Financial problems and worries; stress; lack of time; relationship problems and problem relationships!; business worries and problems; ill-health; fatigue; guilt; jealousy; fear. Isn't it amazing that people are afraid to let go of fear itself; as we've already discussed, they either have to be desperate or ready to wake up.

However, the list of what you gain (all the positives) and what you lose (all the negatives) raises some issues which the normal person has difficulty coming to terms with – for example, "no financial worries". Surely, you may think, I'm not talking about material success, I'm talking about something greater; and, surely, "money is the root of all evil". Yes, I'm talking about a broader, deeper success but that doesn't exclude material success, in fact, it very much includes it.

Let's discuss some of these issues further.

Financial and Material Success

Almost everyone I've ever asked has given "money" as the reason for how they spend their time, what work they do and how hard they work. Most normal people admit to having financial concerns (if not outright worries) and, regardless of how much they have, they never have quite enough. This concern consumes most normal people's minds and in doing so only makes the yearned-for financial security even more elusive. Consider what normal people believe to be a normally successful career. You get a good education (which costs a lot of money) and get a good job. You buy yourself a nice car (to indicate to other people, who really don't care one way or the other about you, that you're successful) which costs a lot of money. You get promoted, or get a bigger better job – so you join the type of clubs where you'll be seen, confirming that, in other people's eyes, you really are climbing the success ladder. You decide it's time to get on that other all-important ladder – the property ladder – and now we're talking serious money. So, as you progress up

to succeed... JUST LET GO

the normal success ladder, your financial needs grow, often beyond your financial resources. You get married and have a couple of children – to whom you'll want to give a top-class education (which costs a lot of money). You'll need to go on the best holidays (it's shocking the number of people who have said to me that they're hung up on the fact that their neighbours go on better holidays!), drive a new, better car, get a second car and, when the time is right, get a bigger, better house, in a better neighbourhood, with a bigger mortgage. You'll also need the other prerequisites of a normally successful life – the right clothes (which cost a lot more than the clothes you need), the right jewellery, the right golf clubs, the right audio system, the latest flat-screen TV, etc., etc. – the list is, literally, endless. When is enough, enough?

Of course, all this show of material wealth gives you something else all normal people crave – standing and recognition. And this, in turn, gives us power – normally over those who have less than we have – or, at least, perceived power. But, then again, isn't everything I've just mentioned about perception rather than reality?

You know the old expression "You can't serve God and money"? Well, that is what this is all about. Normal people have the financial cart before the horse (of living). The world is becoming increasingly obsessed with material wealth and in the process making the winning of that wealth more difficult (the one thing that will stop you getting what you want is trying too hard!) and the end in itself. But that doesn't make the winning of material success wrong or, in some way, contrary to a broader spiritual success. To make matters worse, organised religion has seized on the normal person's perceived need (or greed) and told you that wanting material success is a sin – "It's easier for a camel to go through the eye of a needle than it is for a rich person to enter eternal life!" And yet, at the same time, the book from which I've just quoted, the Bible, states very clearly "If you want something, believe that you have it already and it is given you" or, again, "Ask and you shall receive". However, we're also given a further pointer as to how this works – "Seek first the Kingdom and all these things will be given to you".

Your Goals

What does this mean? Take it from one who sees it in action – and I, in turn, validate this from those of my clients who see it in action in their lives – if you put your living (with a clear mind) before all else, you get what you need financially. To those who let go of the all-consuming desire for financial security, to those who drop out of the all consuming race for financial success, financial success and security simply come to them. Nothing in life comes through effort – because effort implies a lack of belief – everything comes to those who really believe. If you let go (of your obsession with financial security) you will obtain that financial security – without any effort on your part and in greater abundance than you thought possible. This I give you as a fact – a fact of Life.

The problem is normal people won't let go – they think they know best. They think that it is their effort and their focus on financial success that will bring that financial success about. But if you believe yourself to have that success already – if you see yourself already having achieved that success – and, in doing so, go about your daily living with the clarity of mind that I've emphasised again and again in these pages, you'll simply get what you've seen yourself as already having.

Put Life first – your life – and everything else will flow.

Relationships

All the way back in Chapter 2 we talked about how you were programmed in your formative years and how, at some point along the way, someone will tell you they love you – or vice versa. But, normal people actually mean "I love you if…" "I love you if you love me." "I love you if you please me." "I love you because you love me." "I love who I think you are." "I love who I'd like you to be." "I love you because being with you makes me feel good." "I love you if you do what I expect." And then, of course, normal people stop loving (or what they thought was loving). You know the old expression (there are simply so many of them!!!) "Familiarity breeds contempt" – and so it does – the person you're not speaking to at the moment,

to succeed... JUST LET GO

you were in love head-over-heels with at some point. So it is with the person you beat, the person you belittle in front of others, the person you cheat on, the person you lie to, the person you despise. So, what's love and what should you expect from your relationships?

Time for yet another well-worn expression – "Love your neighbour as yourself." But, didn't we agree in Chapter 2 that there's something about us all that we don't like, or would like fixed – that all our personalities are flawed in some way? So, if you don't love yourself you can't love anyone else – at all. But, we also said that your personality isn't you – and by now you know that when I talk about loving yourself, I'm not talking about loving your personality – what's the point, it's not real, it doesn't exist (except in someone else's imagination – what a useless thought!). In your clear state of mind, you feel, you experience the real you – without thoughts, worries, programs, hang-ups – just you. And that perfect you, free from all that garbage, is just that – perfect. Once you realise that (and you can only realise it in a clear state of mind) then all else changes. If your Self – the real you – is perfect, then so is everyone else. But, as a client said to me recently, sometimes it can be really hard – almost impossible – to see the perfection in someone else. And that's true too. There are so many normal people who are so attached to their personality, there isn't a snowball's chance in hell that they'll let go and let the real them out! So, what can you expect from your relationships – expect nothing. Expect nothing from anybody and you'll never be disappointed. But normal people are living in a permanent lather of expectation – and, normally, when it comes to relationships, they are expecting to be made to feel good (or better), accepted, recognised – the normal kind of drugs we discussed before. And, so, normal relationships are a mess.

This might sound harsh – but it's reality. If normal people are mad, and I've set forth enough evidence to strongly suggest they are, then how can normal relationships remotely resemble what a real relationship might be? As a result, following my workshop, some of my clients go home and make up – others go home and break up. What if, in realising how abundant life can be, you also realise that the person you're with is a million miles away from appreciating that

Your Goals

same reality? What if you're living with or married to an "energy snatcher"? The answer is as simple as it is obvious – if you're really all there with them (clear in your mind) you won't see who you're accustomed to thinking you're seeing – you'll see the real person. In turn, because you're all there, your energy might just raise theirs – and the results can by truly magical. But, what if someone is so buried in their thoughts and personality that you can't get through? Well, give everyone a first, second and third chance – but after that, why bother? After all, as we'll see in the next Chapter, your first responsibility is to you.

So, what's love? Unconditional! And in such a climate of unconditional love, what's Life likely to give you? The most spectacular relationships beyond words – where, in clarity of mind, there never is that mind-numbing familiarity, where every now is new. But, don't expect it, don't need it, don't ask for it – just clear your mind and accept it.

Doing Nothing

I mentioned that one of the consequences of real living (with a clear mind) is that you might spend more time doing nothing. In our modern age, this is something with which most people are uncomfortable. We all think we're being lazy if we do nothing – we all feel we should be constantly on the go, constantly striving. And most are decidedly ill-at-ease with the concept that we should actually set aside time for ourselves to simply do nothing. And yet, in doing nothing our minds can be at their stillest – and in that stillness we are closest to our natural state of the spiritual clarity of mind that brings about our perfect life. Very often, we'd be far better off doing nothing than meddling – or struggling, or making an effort – when no such thought-provoked intervention is required at all. Consider the case of Winston Churchill, who I mentioned earlier – what point would energy-wasting running about have been (other than perhaps to have his mind too muddled to be in the right place at the right time and know what he had to do)?

to succeed... JUST LET GO

We are told in all the ancient texts that paint a picture of "paradise" that before we got too obsessed with thought and material success, people spent a lot of their time relaxing, doing nothing other than living abundantly. There's a very powerful message in this for us. You need to have time for yourself – with no-one else involved – to do little or nothing. To go for a walk for the sake of going for a walk (when normal people walk they're rushing to or from somewhere), to sit and watch a beautiful sunset (it's in moments like these that even normal people can get a sense of wonderment) to admire the beauty of where we are – and not to be under any self-imposed pressure to get up and do something else.

The more you clear your mind and the more you move into your natural state of mind of being in the here and now, the more you will find yourself experiencing these wonderful moments of doing nothing. For a long time, I will admit I felt guilty when I caught myself enjoying such a moment – but that's only thought, thinking that I should be doing something or that I'm wasting time.

More Detachment!

Before we actually move on to your visualisation and description of your own goals, it is vital that you bear one important fact in mind. From years of living in a programmed way, in a programmed world where exceptional success is seen as unattainable by normal people, your ideas about your perfect life can be nothing other than incomplete – or seriously short of the abundance that Life has in store for you. From your programmed perspective, you don't know what's best for you – I don't know what's best for me, hence a whole chapter on letting go!

In your aspiring towards your future goals, I propose that you *prefer* – not want or need. As I say to my wife – and she says to me – "I don't need you – but I very much prefer to have you around." If your happiness or your view of success depends on a particular outcome, you're setting yourself up!

Your Goals

You need to stay detached from any particular outcome – detach yourself from everything other than the clarity of mind of living in the here and now – and what you'll get in return for your putting your clarity of mind first might well astound you – I know it's astounded me.

So, in framing your goals or your view of your ideal life, the less specific you are about what you prefer to have or be doing, the more you will realise exactly what it is that gives you your perfect life.

Your Success

We're all unique. There are things that only you can do and there are people whose lives only you can touch. This is why it is so important that you wake up, free your mind and ensure that you fulfil your potential – because if you don't do what only you can do no-one else will. And, if there are others depending on you to wake up – if you don't, who'll change their lives? The other consequence of this is that you – and you only – can define your success. I can only set out the few pointers that I have – but now you've got to decide what it is you prefer from Life.

In performing this task, the following questions might well focus your mind:

- If you were told that you've got only one more month to live, how would you spend the time allotted to you?

- If you had no financial concerns whatsoever, how would you spend your time?

- If you were totally carefree, describe how you'd spend your perfect day – where would you be, who would you be with, what would you be doing?

Of course, by this point, I hope you've noticed that the three questions deliberately focus on how we all can live our lives to the

to succeed... JUST LET GO

full, by living in clarity of mind, without any worries or concerns – in fact, being carefree.

Don't just give the three questions some casual thought – we know how dangerous casual thought can be! In Chapter 12 I suggest you buy a special book in which you can write – your Life Book. Maybe this would be a good time to start writing. But, just for now, write what comes into your head, what feels right, without having to think about it at all – just jot it down as it comes out.

The important thing, at this point, is that you start defining your success – no holds barred, without any limitations. Consider what you would do "if only" – because if only, rather than not-too-bad, is what you're meant to be doing, what you're entitled to and, quite probably, the things that only you can do – with the people only you can touch. So answer those three questions from the perspective of "too-good-to-be-true" – after all, all the mystics and spiritualists through the ages tell us that the life too-good-to-be-true is the life you're meant to live.

Setting Your Mind

All you have to do now is set your mind to the task! Your subconscious mind is cybernetic – just like a heat-seeking missile. So, if you prefer to achieve something that you don't already have or which you currently believe to be unachievable, you simply set your mind by taking a photograph of your preferred goal – in just the same way that your mind took its original photographs when you were a child. You take your chosen photograph in the completely clear state of mind that you experience through the mental exercises in this book. When you set your mind by taking your photograph, you then just leave your mind to do what it does best – create your world from your programs (that's what it's been doing all along anyway). Your mind will go around this way and that to get to its destination, but it will end up getting to there, if you leave your mind to do the job. And you leave your mind to its own devices by keeping your mind clear. In this way, your clear mind can best communicate with universal

Your Goals

energy and bring about what it is you prefer. Now, if you're going to set your mind by having it take a photograph, the first thing you need to do is describe that photograph.

Describing Your Goals – To Your Self

Let's consider the third question again – "If you were totally carefree, describe how you'd spend your perfect day – where would you be, who would you be with, what would you be doing?" If, as I hope, you have jotted down the points that popped into your head, then, at this point, you have your list of ingredients – now, it's time to bake the cake!

Describe your perfect day to your Self in words that your true Self, your subconscious mind, understands. Use the five representational systems – see, feel, hear, smell and taste the experience of your perfect day – and do so in the present tense, as if you're actually there experiencing it now. Remember, "If you want something, believe you have it already and it is given to you" – this is how this works in practice.

Let me give you an example from one of my clients, as many of my clients would describe perfect days with broad similarities. For the sake of understanding, the client involved is married to Sylvie and has three children, Alan, Charlotte and Candice.

I'm standing beside the swimming pool – I can see the crystal blue of the water and the way the sun breaks into pieces on the water's surface. I feel the ice-cold condensation on the bottle of beer in my hand as I smell the smoke rising off the barbecue. The steaks are sizzling and smoking and spitting in all directions as I turn them. I cast my eye across the stunning mixture of colours that lie before me – the dazzling white of the villa, the deep greens of the creeper's leaves, the vibrant purples of the bougainvillea – wow, I take a deep breath and smell the heady mixture of the scent from its flowers, mixed with the smoke and sizzling meat on the barbecue, the sweaty

to succeed... JUST LET GO

smells of the heat of the day, the sun cream, the pine trees in the background. I take a big gulp of ice-cold beer – and let it sparkle on my tongue, as if I can feel the liquid dance on each of my taste buds. My head is turned by the screaming and splashing of the kids as they dive into the pool – their glistening brown bodies, their wet hair, the hysterical laughing and splashing. Charlotte hauls herself out, dripping and dives back in with a loud boom, submerging the others under a tidal wave – a wave of laughter and happiness. I feel the heat of the sun embrace me – its not too hot, it is just so comfortable to stand here, cooking lunch, wrapped in this heat. I look up into a deep blue sky – hazy with the mixture of the midday heat, the smoke from the barbecue and the energy rising off the trees. I look at Sylvie, I notice her body, her curves. I look deep into her eyes – as if for the first time – and we smile. I feel a deep sense of excitement and love somewhere inside me. I turn the steaks again – they spit onto my arm and the smoke rises into my face. The kids are going wilder now, their laughter beyond control, so contagious that we all start laughing – in the heat, the joy, the love of this superb moment. I call to Sylvie and the kids – lunch is served – I walk across the grass, I can feel each blade caress the soles of my feet, on to the patio where the heat of the sun makes the concrete almost ignite my feet – the kids come running to the table, I look at each of them in turn, we sit down, admire the food, smell it – and taste it – wow.

The foregoing is nothing more than an example – but it gives you a feel for what we're trying to achieve here. Notice a couple of things – he didn't say that he was free from worries – he didn't need to, it was implied in the complete carefreeness of the moment. He didn't say he had no financial concerns – again it was already done. He didn't say he only works four hours a day, three days a week and goes on many holidays such as this one – he didn't need to, it was implied. The picture he painted for himself pre-supposed that all these minor details were all already looked after. He also kept going over and back over the various senses – seeing, feeling, hearing, smelling,

Your Goals

tasting, feeling, hearing, seeing, smelling, seeing, tasting – this is how you wrap your mind up in the five representational systems, how you excite your mind into the desired moment.

Remember, your subconscious mind is like a child's mind, the bigger the impression you can make on it, the more exciting you can make it, the more attention your mind pays it. Your picture must excite you – unlike one of my clients who, on his first attempt, suggested that one of his main goals was that he'd have no mortgage – how exciting can that be! Go on, excite yourself.

Write It Down

Now, you're going to write down your perfect day, in your Book of Life – you're going to write the whole scene, as an essay, which describes the whole picture before you, of your perfect day, as you see, feel, hear, smell and taste what you already have. The effort of writing your essay, in the present tense, describing what your five senses are experiencing here and now unlocks the gateway to your subconscious mind and brings you into that clarity of mind in that moment you're describing in writing. By the time you've finished, you've written what you already have.

Taking the Picture

To top it all off, you can now allow your subconscious mind to take your picture of your perfect day. Remember, your film isn't loaded and your flash isn't switched on until you're in a clear state of mind. So, like all the earlier exercises in this book, you must start by gradually lowering yourself into that clear state of mind. Then, when you're in that clarity of mind, you walk into the picture that you've described for yourself in writing and you see, feel, hear, smell and taste the experience. Here are the steps:

to succeed... JUST LET GO

1. Sitting upright, put your feet firmly on the floor, hands on your legs.

2. Whenever you feel comfortable, let your eyes gently close.

3. Listen and notice all of the sounds you hear. Notice that each sound becomes clearer, you can even notice the quietest of sounds.

4. Focus on each of your breaths individually – each breath in and each breath out brings you to a deeper level of relaxation and clears your mind further.

5. Refocus your attention to each sound you hear and then back to your breathing, mixing between the sounds and your breath, until you are completely and deeply relaxed.

6. See yourself stepping into your picture and see what it's like to be there – looking out through your own eyes, rather than looking at yourself in the picture.

7. Take your time to see all your surroundings, the texture of what you see, the vibrancy of the colours that you see – as if each colour and texture were new to you. Take your time to look in detail at the other people here with you – their features, how they look, look into their eyes.

8. Hear all the sounds associated with what's happening – notice how clear the sounds are.

9. Feel what it's like to be here – the heat (or cold), the breeze, the log fire – whatever sensations give you a feeling of being here. Feel the grass or carpet under your feet. Feel the armchair, the bottle or glass in your hand, take care to notice each feeling individually.

10. Now, feel what it's like to be here, emotionally – the wonderful feeling of warmth, peace, joy and happiness. In doing so, again notice who else is with you, how you feel

Your Goals

towards them – and how you feel in the wonderful surroundings you see around you.

11. Taste the drink or food in your mouth – smell the log fire, the food cooking, the pine scent of the forest – whatever it is where you are.

12. Repeat steps 7 to 11 many times over, so as to wrap yourself up in the total sensual experience of being in this moment here now.

13. In your own good time, bring yourself back to your breathing – count your breaths, in and out and, whenever you're ready, open your eyes.

What's Next?

The short answer is "nothing"! But, there's a longer answer to explain that "nothing". In life and in business, you were taught, up to now, that if you want to get to position X you sketch out what it might be like to be there as compared to where you are at the moment and then you'll give yourself a series of milestones along the way, position B, C and so on. From this you'll prepare your action plan, your long-term action plan and your short-term action plan. And, of course, when you build up your short-term action plan you might just realise that position X may not be attainable at all. That's the way you've been taught to plan and that's also the way businesses plan their strategy.

Dave preferred to live in a big white house with a red roof (and, by the way, now does!). After he'd described it to himself, after he'd written his "essay" and after he'd taken his picture of himself sitting on the patio of the big white house, he said to me, "Now do I have to write down the steps I have to take to get there?" I said, "What will happen if you write down step one?" He said, "I'll realise that I don't have the money that I need to get that house." I asked him, "And

to succeed... JUST LET GO

what's the consequence of that?" He answered, "The goal is ridiculous!" And once you think that the goal is ridiculous, it is.

By now, I hope you realise that logical thought (and we haven't mentioned bad words like this for a while) has no place in living life to the full. Logical thought stops living in its tracks. Simply discard the notion that you have to do anything at all after you've taken the steps described in this chapter, because, in taking further steps, you're implying that you don't fully believe that you've already got your picture. And one of the worst things you could do is wonder when all this will happen – or worry why nothing appears to have happened yet. Now you do know they're useless thoughts, don't you?

Clarity of Mind

And so, what you need to do after you've taken your picture is go about what it is you have to do now, in a clear state of mind. As far as your subconscious mind is concerned, your goal, your picture has already been achieved; it believes it, because it has that picture of you enjoying yourself in that perfect place already in its album, it is a program that it is now running – but this time it's your program, this time you're in control. And, we've already discussed how clarity of mind will tune you in to the synchronicity and opportunities that already abound around you. So this clarity of mind will enable you to do what feels right to bring about your perfect picture. You, through applying logical thought, haven't the first clue how best to achieve your goal but your subconscious mind knows what best to do instinctively – so let it do what it does best. You stay out of the way! Hence my continuing emphasis on clarity of mind. It's not only the state of mind you must be in to take the pictures you want it is also the state of mind you must maintain to enable your subconscious mind to bring about the achievement of all of your goals. Put clarity of mind, living in the now, first – and everything else flows. There is nothing more important than your clarity of mind.

Your Goals

The Greatest Goal of All

Before we finish this chapter, you might consider setting your mind to the achievement of the greatest goal of all – that of simply living life to the full, without any of the preconditions that, undoubtedly, even your preferences are. By taking your photograph of your perfect day you have taken control – nevertheless, you are still in a PlayStation game, although, at least, now you have the controls! What about stepping outside the PlayStation game altogether? That's letting go. And, as we discussed in Chapter 10, when you let go, without any preconditions, your life will become even more abundant than you could imagine in your wildest dreams. As I said before, I know this as a fact that I experience daily – and I can verify it through the experiences of some of my clients who have let go also.

In setting your mind to simply live life to the full, by living in clarity of mind, quite literally "God knows" what will happen – and so you embark on an effortless journey of discovery and abundance. Put Life first and everything else falls into place – effortlessly.

Chapter Summary

- Success is effortless happiness, contentment, peace and plenty in every aspect of your life.

- It is your birthright to live stress-free – with no financial concerns, wonderful unconditional relationships and plenty of time to do what you love doing.

- In defining your success, need nothing and want nothing.

- Making your success dependant on certain prerequisites gives those needs and wants the power to make you both happy and unhappy. Let your goals be nothing more than preferences – detach yourself from all specific outcomes.

to succeed... JUST LET GO

- To define your success, focus on the three key questions asked of you in this chapter.

- You then set your mind to the achievement of your preferences by:

  - Describing what you see, feel, hear, smell and taste experiencing your perfect day, as if you're already there.

  - Writing down a detailed "essay" describing your experience in the present tense, again using your five representational systems.

  - Taking your photograph of your perfect day - again focusing on the use of all your senses, having first relaxed yourself into a deep state of clarity of mind.

- After that you do not question when, how or if this goal is going to be achieved – you focus on living in a clear state of mind, doing what you're doing at each moment of each day.

- This clarity of mind will enable your subconscious mind to be most effective in bringing about the achievement of your preferences.

- This clarity of mind also enables your subconscious mind to bring about even better results than your preferences, if you let go of all preferences and simply focus on living in that clear state of mind – putting Life first and letting everything happen for you.

Chapter Twelve
Take Responsibility

Normal people grow old, they don't grow up. They are not prepared to be responsible for their own actions because, in fact, they reactbased on their programs and their useless thoughts. They are not prepared to take responsibility for their own lives, choosing instead to look to others to lay the blame for their inability to achieve their goals. "My boss doesn't like me, how could I possibly get promoted!" "The system's unfair." "The odds are stacked against me" – whatever the odds are!? "My wife's an alcoholic." "My husband beats me." "My children don't care." "My religion says that I should hate you." "How could I have got that job – they think I'm too old?" "I had to screw my colleague at work – that's the way the system works." "What would the others think of me if I didn't put him in his place." Normal people's lives, if that's really what we should call them at all, are a series of excuses, built from a series of programs – their personalities – that most normal people are proud to call themselves.

Time to Wake Up

No book will make you wake up and take responsibility. This book won't. The others you may have read exhorting you to get a life won't do it either. Nothing and no-one will do this for you – you're on your own. And whether you like it or not, it's always been this way anyway, it's just that normal people will distract themselves with their new

to succeed... JUST LET GO

car, their new home, drink, drugs, sex and holidays to avoid having to face up to this reality. You're responsible for yourself – you either grasp that liberating opportunity or you stay dead. It is time to grow up or go to hell – your own personal version of hell. There's nothing in between – heaven or hell – the choice is yours. And all it takes is for you to say yes in every now from now on. Maybe that sounds too good to be true. But, it only sounds too good to be true, because, for all the years of your life up to now, you were told something different.

So, I'm asking you, do you want to take responsibility for yourself? Do you want to put clarity of mind ahead of worry, concern, stress? This is actually a question to which there is only one logical answer – perhaps the first time that logic has been useful!

Making the Change

All you have to do is be alert – to ensure that your mind is free as much as possible. We all have bad days, the odd mood swing even, but as long as we can be alert to these minor distractions, see them for what they are and return to clarity of mind, then, that's all that's required. It is that simple – but because no-one's ever told you this before, you find it difficult to accept its simplicity. But, to quote Mahatma Gandhi, you must be the change that you wish to see. And you do this by simply ensuring that your mind stays clear.

A couple of my clients have said to me that they have no difficulty experiencing this clarity of mind – they say they "escape" regularly; one has a wonderful time fishing, whilst another plays the guitar. I've asked them both, why would you choose to escape for such brief periods and then return to the prison cell of your daily life? Why not free your mind completely and enjoy yourself all of the time? In exactly the same way, it intrigues me how normal people live it up for two to three weeks each year – and play dead for the rest of the year. The whole concept of holiday seems to be part of the con that has been perpetrated on normal people. Indeed, when my wife says to me that she feels as if she's on holiday all of the time, we agree that that's how life is meant to be.

Take Responsibility

You're meant to be living life to the full, meant to be happy, meant to be relaxed all of the time. Given the choice between the kind of life I've just described and the zombie half-life that normal people live – do you have a choice?

To make the change you simply need to commit yourself to keeping your mind clear – to stay in constant touch with your Self. That's how you make the change.

The Hell That Otherwise Awaits

Most normal people are not in hell (although some of them clearly are) – they are in the world of not-too-bad. But what if you know and grasp the contents of this book and simply keep existing in the world of not-too-bad? In reading this book, you've opened a doorway into the real world. But an opened door can either be entered – as I am suggesting you do – or can let in a draught, and a very stiff one at that. It is my experience and that of many of my clients that, once knowing the abundance that Life makes available to us, if we let ourselves drift back into not-too-bad, you'll suffer more than ever. Not-too-bad becomes not-too-worse for the slob who's so lazy that they won't set a couple of minutes aside each day to continually improve their clarity of mind skills. Armed with the knowledge that your life is meant to be amazingly successful in every way, you are tempting fate, so to speak, if you do nothing about accepting the abundance that is yours by right.

So, this book may well open the door. But, as I have said already, only you can walk through it!

Practical Steps to Taking Responsibility

There is a whole world of difference between intellectually understanding the content of this book and actually living in the manner proposed. So, what can you do differently that will make the difference? The answer, of course, should be obvious by now – you

to succeed... JUST LET GO

live with a clear mind. Remember that clarity of mind is your natural state – you don't have to learn anything new. You don't even have to unlearn all the nonsense that has clogged your mind – you simply drop it all by keeping your mind clear. But what practical steps should you take to enable you to do this?

I would suggest that you set aside five minutes, a couple of times a day, to do some of the exercises in this book. You should set your mind each morning in exactly the same way that you wash and get dressed – after all, if you wouldn't consider leaving the house naked, why would you set out without being mentally prepared? But deliberately set your mind on awake – rather than pretending you're doing an exercise before you get out of bed, you must deliberately sit upright and do the drill!

If you drive to work, then drive with the radio or CD player off – turn yourself on instead and tune into the station of Life! Deliberately practice the "Driving Clarity of Mind Exercise" from Chapter 6 – see, feel, hear, smell and taste all the wonderous things going on in the daily rush-hour. One of the main things you'll notice is how dead the expression is on all the other drivers' faces! Anyway, what will you have missed on the radio? News reports that simply confirm and reconfirm that the world is, at best, not-too-bad, at worst, that lunatics in various parts of the world are murdering each other, driven Hell-bent by the programs they don't even know they have. Alternatively, you'll miss the early morning show that plays wall-to-wall music, distraction for the feeble-minded. As an important aside, I am not deriding music – it can be one of the most stirring and, at the same time, most relaxing creations we have available to us. But, if you want to listen to music, set time aside to listen to it – don't do it when you're supposed to be doing something else.

If you get the bus or train to work – then look around you, see where you are, see who else is with you – most are not all there! Stay alert, watch out for the coincidences. Again, the first thing you'll notice is how dead everyone else looks. And, if you walk to work, what a wonderful opportunity to focus your mind on the bodily exertion, what and who you see, etc., etc.

Take Responsibility

Don't – ever – rush your meals. Make and take the time to savour what you're eating or drinking, even it happens to be a cup of coffee or glass of water. Don't ever dismiss anyone too hastily – one of them might be the person who changes your life. Make time to do one of your clarity of mind exercises during the working day – you'll find the best place and most opportune time if you really want to! And don't seek out silence, there's no such thing in the world as auditory silence. In any event, it's the silence within that you're seeking.

When you come home in the evening, come home. Make sure all of you comes through the front (or side) door – there may be people at home to whom your homecoming is one of the most important events of their day or life. And, as you know, if one of them is your young child, he or she will know straight away if you've fully arrived or if you're there in body only. Again, take time for the evening meal and don't have the TV on while you're eating, you'll be missing one of the most important opportunities you have to practise your clarity of mind, by really being there, seeing, tasting and smelling the food, seeing and hearing what the others are saying and feeling just how good it is to be alive – really alive.

Make sure you set time aside each evening for another clarity of mind exercise – even if you've ten children under five years of age, you'll find the best place and the opportune time, if you really want to. And make sure you do nothing during some part of the day – nothing at all other than being wherever you are. Cut out some of modern so-called living's worst habits – texting on your mobile (how many pubs have I been in where there are ten young people sitting around a table and none of them is there – they're all texting, sometimes each other!); channel-hopping on the television (the TV being perhaps this and the last century's most potent and underestimated drug). I'm not suggesting you throw your television out, I'm simply suggesting that you control it, not the other way around. Reading the newspapers can seriously damage your health as well. You may need your newspaper from a work or professional perspective but it's amazing how many people rush headlong to work to be in early each morning, spend the first forty minutes reading the paper and then wonder how they get so little done. However, good news is not news

to succeed... JUST LET GO

at all – the papers are not only full of program-fulfilling stories that life is not-too-bad, the papers actually revel in the worst news possible. Where would journalists be without wars, terrorists, political scandal, sexual scandal, financial scandal, business scandal, accidents, fatalities or natural disasters. And then there are the sports pages! But that's OK as long as you don't take it too seriously.

Don't look forward to anything – when it happens, it happens. And don't dwell in the past – but don't discard it, your memories might be all you have of people near and dear. Don't forget that "shit happens" – but as all the great mystics tell us, whatever happens, happens. You just get on with staying clear in your mind and doing what you're doing. Also, don't forget that your mind will wander – you can be absolutely certain of that – the key issue is what you will do when your mind wanders. You will start worrying – again a certainty (one of my clients called me one day to tell me he was worried that he had nothing to worry about!) – the key issue is, will you continue to worry once you've started?

If you do a couple of exercises a day and take every opportunity during the day to keep your mind clear, you will be alert enough to stop your mind when it starts to wander, stop worrying when you start and notice the useless thoughts once they creep up on you. All of this is done by simply coming to your senses again – seeing, feeling, tasting, hearing and smelling where you are. And, having done that couple of exercises each day, you will be alert enough to notice those people and events that are staring you in the face as opportunities to move your own life along towards your bigger goals. The key is not just to wake up (and then fall asleep again) but to stay awake.

And never get disheartened – thinking about that is a completely useless thought. If you find yourself beating yourself up over something you have or haven't done, forget it, come back to your five senses and clear your mind afresh. I am suggesting that you don't blame yourself – but that you take full responsibility for yourself. No-one else will.

Take Responsibility

What About Your Personality?

Your personality has ruled – and ruined – your life up to now. Even if you already consider yourself to be successful, you've only scratched the surface of your true potential. But, as we already know, your true potential will never be reached either by your personality or, more pointedly, whilst your personality is in the way. So you need to forget who you thought you were too. If you're fully clear in your mind, this simply happens – a clear mind is a personality-free mind and one that clears the way for the magic to happen.

Are you big enough to drop your personality? You know, you really do have to lose your life to find it. Are you ready to discard the world of not-too-bad in return for unlimited abundance? You don't need to think about your answer, you simply need to keep your mind clear.

And Finally

Only you can save yourself and you cannot save anyone else until you save yourself first. Saying or thinking that you love your husband, wife, partner or children, whilst existing in the world of not-too-bad with a muddled mind is a lie. You are no use to anyone until you wake up – you are a waste of energy until you come to your senses. You will drag those you claim to love to Hell with you, if you don't wake up. I'm not blaming you – the normal world has stacked all the cards against you – I'm asking you to take responsibility.

Chapter Summary

- Normal people are irresponsible people – and the world is the worse for it.

- Only you can be responsible for you – if you don't embrace that responsibility your life won't just stay not-too-bad, it will get worse.

to succeed... JUST LET GO

- You must go about your day ensuring that you take every opportunity to practise your newly remembered skills of living with a clear mind.

- You must set aside enough time each day to practise a couple of the exercises in this book.

- You must be ever watchful for the occasions when your mind wanders, when you worry or when your personality tries to regain control.

- You must constantly be alert – ensuring that you keep bringing yourself back to your senses.

- If you don't save yourself no-one else will – not only will you squander the opportunity for abundant living, but you'll ensure that those you claim to love never get a fair chance at it either.

Chapter Thirteen
Start Living

You are a creator of your world – what your subconscious mind believes is manifest in the physical world. As you know by now, this is how everyone's life is led anyway. You also now know that it is totally within your power to create the world that you want. But, as you also know, the world you want might not be the best for you or for others. For example, Adolf Hitler was completely single-minded in creating his world, but not everyone would agree that it was a perfect one. As we discussed in the last couple of chapters, your best bet is to set your mind to a non-specific goal or a goal of just letting go altogether. In this way, you let Life look after you; you enter into the flow – the fast-flowing river of Life.

The Journey

You know the well-worn expression "God only knows!" – well, that's how you could best embark upon this amazing journey of discovery. You discover how effortless success can be. You discover your own innate power and wisdom. You discover that you depend on nobody else – for anything. You discover that Life, God or universal energy (decide which description suits you best) gives to you abundantly, without you even asking.

It doesn't matter how successful you currently are; even if you're already a huge success, you've really only scratched the surface. Business success, financial success, material success, successful

to succeed... JUST LET GO

relationships, a wonderful – and wonder-full – personal life is yours. All you have to do is put Life first and ask Life to let you have what's yours by right. I know – this is the Life that I lead. Some of my clients know – this is the Life that they lead. (I wish that all of my clients would know – but they still have to take their responsibility.)

Be Selfish

I urge you to be selfish in the pursuit of your birthright of unlimited success. I mean good-selfish, not the way normal people interpret that word. Put your Self, that is the real you without programs and thoughts, beyond your personality – first. You know the real you, the one you are in that clear state of mind. Put your Self first and the whole world becomes a different place. Suddenly you are free of limiting thought, you are free to notice your gut feelings – your intuitions – you are free to notice the coincidences that will change your life and you are free to be here, in the here and now. And, being free to be here, now, means that you're all here for everyone else too.

You know, one of the most selfish things that you could do is be nice to other people, just for the sake of being nice – without expecting anything in return. In so doing, you raise others' energy, they start noticing too and you further heighten the whole process of coincidence, opportunity and synchronicity. And even though, as I said earlier, you should expect nothing from anybody (so that you won't be disappointed), what goes around really does come around – in opening up to others, you get back a hundred times over. And I'm not just talking about being nice to the people you like (which of course is looking at those people through the thought of "I like them") – I include everyone in this. The well-worn expression "Love your enemies" springs to mind. You get what you give – often not from the person you gave to – but that's how Life works.

Put your Self first all of the time – because if you're all here, you make a difference to people and, boy, do they notice. If you've young children, there's no point in putting them first if you're

Start Living

uncomfortable with who you think you are (your personality) – there's no-one more capable than a young child to see through the nonsense of so-called adults. If you're clear, if you're really here, then that in itself enables you raise the energy of your children too.

Let the Success Flow

Living with a free mind leaves you clear to follow your gut feelings, to do things you might not otherwise have done, to talk to people you might otherwise never dream of approaching. You don't know who will be the next person to enter your life and change it but, with an open mind, not only will you spot them, you will follow up on it. In this way, your success – and the success that is everyone else's by right as well – flows.

You will meet and do business with people that your logical mind could never have dreamed of – or have countenanced. You will have relationships with people who you meet casually (isn't that how you met your "nearest and dearest" anyway) but who a normal person, so buried in thought, would totally ignore. These opportunities – noticed and taken – will lead you to places you could not imagine. I know. This is the Life I live – and so do some of my clients!

My clients often ask me, "Does this mean I'll leave my job and find myself doing something different?" The answer! it's different for everybody. The forgotten wisdom contained in this book results in some people doing completely different things, in completely different places, sometimes with completely different people than they would or could have ever imagined. For others, they're still doing exactly the same as always – except nowadays, they're actually doing what they're doing! This is about living our ordinary lives extraordinarily – and that's understating just how exceptional life this way is.

to succeed... JUST LET GO

Life is Not a Competition

I know you've been told otherwise – at school, in exams, on the field of play, at work, in the boardroom and, though few normal people would be prepared to admit it, at home. Life is not a competition – you are here first of all, to, be here and, in being here, help others be a little more all there too. Don't get me wrong, when you play a competitive sport, you play to win. When you manoeuvre your way around the office politics, you do so with a purpose. But realise this important truth – they're all the games that people play. Business is just a game – Life is real. And Life is the only thing that is real.

But, of course, in your clear state of mind, you know this to be true. And you know when to play and how to play those games. In doing so, from the position of the unlimited strength that is the real you – you cannot but win. But the real paradox – that normal people cannot handle at all – is that when the real you wins, no-one loses. It's what a consultant friend of mine calls a Win-Win situation!

Shining Your Light

So you're actually here to raise the dead – to help everyone else to wake up as well! That's why I said you need to be selfish – because you'll only be useful to others when you're all here yourself. I've quoted Nelson Mandela before and now's a good time to do it again. He says, "There is nothing enlightening about shrinking so that others won't feel insecure around you. We are all meant to shine, as children do; we are born to manifest the Glory of God that is within us. It is not just in some of us – it is in everyone."

Shine your light – be all here for yourself and for everyone. A couple of your friends, family, acquaintances, they might notice – they might start shining their light too. Spread the word, not by preaching, not by saying but by doing, by being – in the here and now. You might just make the difference to someone else – perhaps, someone who matters. But, I've said "perhaps" because only they can take responsibility for themselves.

Start Living

With a clear mind, you don't even need to consider what I've just said; with a clear mind you're here – in the here and now – you have presence and others notice presence!

Heaven

And so Life, God, universal energy – call it what you will – begins to fashion your own heaven, right here, right now. You know now that you don't wait until you die for the heaven that you've been told about. Your clarity of mind and the success it automatically and inevitably creates gives you heaven, here, now. And this is your natural state of mind, your natural way of living – and your God-given birthright.

You were created perfectly, you are a child of God. You are here to live life and live life to the full, you're not here to worry about anything, because, if you put your Self, which is Life, first, everything else is given to you. It is as black and white, and as simple as that.